CH 7199. 538
258

D1297812

CH 7199. 538
258

THE SCULPTORS

O'CONNOR

Picture Credits:
Calvin Jones. Holden, Massachusetts. Extensive photographic work.
Donald Stinson. Skaneateles, N.Y. - Loney Tomb.
D.C. French - Chesterwood Museum, Stockbridge, MA. - O'Connor Sr.
Cemetery Monument.
Scott Wiggins. St. Paul, Minnesota. Governor John Johnson & Toilers.
James Cheever. Annapolis Naval Academy. Bust of Commodore Barry.
Corcoran Gallery of Art. Adam & Eve, Gift of Edward Tuck.Washington.DC.
Photographs by Winthrop, Portrait specialists. W.Boylston, MA.
Studio Dick Brouwer bv. Picture of Justice at Hague, Netherlands.

The Sculptors O'Connor. Copyright @ 1995 by Doris Soderman.
Printed and bound in the United States of America. All rights reserved. No part
of this book may be reproduced in any form or by any electronic or mechanical
means including information storage and retrieval systems without permission in
writing from the publisher, except by a reviewer, who may quote brief passages
in a review. Published by Gundi Publishers, Box #820
1102 Pleasant Street, Worcester, Massachusetts.01602

First printing 1995.
Although the author and publisher have exhaustively researched all sources to ensure the
accuracy and completeness of the information contained in this book, we assume no
responsibility for errors, inaccuracies, omissions or any inconsistency herein. Any slights of
people or organizations are unintnentional..Readers should consult an attorney or accoun-
tant for specific applications to their individual publishing ventures.

Library of Congress Cataloging in Publication   # 94-078620.
ISBN 0 - 9642863-0-0 hard cover,   0-9642863-3-5. Softcover.
O'Connor, Andrew Sr. 1847 - 1924. Andrew Jr. 1874 - 1941.
Biography.

Gundi Publishers
Box #820
1102 Pleasant Street
Worcester, MA. 01602.
(508) 757-8940

Printed in the United States of America
by Quebecor Printing, Kingsport, Tenn.

The Sculptors O'Connor

Andrew Sr. 1847 - 1924

Andrew Jr.   1874 - 1941

By Doris Flodin Soderman.

Dedicated To

Larry, Lenore, and Emily.

Contents

INTRODUCTION:

The idea of a biography of Andrew O'Connor was conceived in 1965 when my husband and I bought the former O'Connor property in Paxton, Massachusetts. The previous owners were Chip and Ginny Fay who along with the legal documents involved in the sale, handed us a sheaf of papers and suggested I become acquainted with the O'Connor family who had lived on the property from 1915 to 1925. The brief history had been written by Elizabeth Rozzell Fay, Chip's mother. After reading her notes with great interest, I put the papers away with the thought that someday researching them would be fun to do.

Except for the house, stable and five acres surrounding them, the forty five acres included in the property, was surveyed and cut into lots of twenty five by one hundred feet. In a scheme designed to make money for the owner, all the land was sold to a Worcester theatre located a half hour away in terms of transportation at that time. The theatre then ran a promotional where one lucky ticket a week was drawn and the owner of it given a twenty five foot lot with the stipulation that he buy three more in order to build a house.

Although today Paxton is thought of as one of the wealthier suburbs of Worcester, Massachusetts, at that time it was a farming community in no-wheres-ville. The Depression deepened, and the lucky people who had won land in the hills of Paxton, suddenly found that there were yearly taxes due on it. Times were not good and the mere pittance that the Town charged was more than most movie goers could afford. Gradually, most of the land was seized by the Town for non-payment of taxes.

When the money making scheme for the land fizzled, the studio on the original acreage was razed, and the lumber presumably sold. Shortly thereafter, the house burned to the ground, leaving an open cellar and the original stable that O'Connor used briefly as his studio when he moved there.

In 1948 my husband and I built one of the first homes on the surveyed property that by now was being sold in four-lot segments by the Town of Paxton. Our only neighbors were the Fay family who had converted the stable into a snug, cozy home on the side of a hill.

World War II was over and by the 1950's the returning soldiers were marrying and looking for land on which they could build, and the neighborhood grew quickly.

Our children became close friends with the Fay children, and therefore when the Fays had to sell their home, we immediately purchased it, coveting the land that surrounded it.

As with previous owners, Chip and Ginny were reluctant to move, for there is a quality about this small piece of real estate that fosters an overwhelming love for it. We soon discovered that we never felt like owners, but only caretakers of this special place for the time we live here.

Almost thirty years later, I began to research O'Connor's work and became fascinated with his story. I had wondered why he was not known in his own country, and perhaps after reading his biography it may be understandable. I have felt his presence many times, helping with this task, and sincerely hope that somewhere he is satisfied with the final results.

Andrew O'Connor Jr. in his twenties.

I

The Early Years

When Andrew O'Connor Sr. died in 1924, his eldest son, Andrew Jr., lost not only his father, but his mentor, teacher and confidante. Although the father loved all of his children, he recognized that his eldest son, Andrew Jr., had an artistic talent that needed more time and encouragement than the others. This was the seed of Andrew O'Connor Jr.'s career as a sculptor..

O'Connor Sr. was born at the home of his maternal parents in Lanarkshire, Scotland in 1846. There were few doctors, and midwives delivered babies, so Jeane Darrach O'Connor felt safer going home to her parents to deliver her child. After a short time, her husband, Owen, brought Jeane and little Andrew back home to County Cavan, Ireland. In the 1840's, Ireland was a very difficult place in which to live. The people were frustrated by the high rents that were assessed by absent English landlords. The rents were continually being raised, and when the time came that a tenant could not pay, he was thrown into the street with his belongings and forced to find other meager accomodations. There were two main crops grown in Ireland at this time, corn and potatoes. When the farmers finally had to export the corn to pay their bills, they subsisted on potatoes. As long as this crop was abundant, they survived, although nutrition-wise it was not adequate.

A potato blight causing great famine occurred in the years of eighteen forty five, six and seven, and people were dying by the tens of thousands from starvation and diseases of malnutrition, cholera and dysentery. This was the beginning of the large scale emigration to America.

In 1850, Owen and Jeane decided to seek a better llife for themselves than they faced in Ireland and with little Andrew, joined two hundred thousand other emigrants to America. They had relatives in Providence, Rhode Island, and found a warm welcome there, and help to become acclimated and find work.

Andrew attended public school where, in the upper grades, his studies included modeling and carving. As he became older he worked in the Providence Art School, developing his natural inclination toward art. He eventually found work with a marble cutter and mastered the trade. Eager to grow in this medium, he wanted to learn the art of sculpture and figure work, but had no financial resources to pursue this path.

In 1872 at the age of twenty six, Andrew married Mary Ella Mcfadden, twenty, who bore his first child, Andrew Jr.on July 7, 1874. Although they had moved to Worcester, Massachusetts, where there was ample work in the field of marble cutting, the child was born at the home of relatives in Providence. When Mary Ella and the baby were in sufficiently good shape to move, Andrew Sr. took them back to Worcester where they took residence in a boarding house on Southbridge Street. O'Connor worked as a marble cutter on Central Street where there were several establishments involved in the same business. He knew his art well and never worried about finding work.

For three years O'Connor had worked at the same place, but as time went on he found he could get better pay down the street and therefore changed jobs. He had been saving as much money as he could with hopes of furthering his education. He theorized that if he could learn sculpting he would be happier and the pay would, of course, be better. There were few sculptors in the country in the 1870's and Andrew O'Connor Sr. wanted desperately to be one of them.

Moving from place to place began at an early age for O'Connor Jr. and throughout most of his life, the moves occurred due to financial reasons. The year that Andrew Jr. turned three, they packed their belongings and took the boat for Florence, Italy. Florence, at the end of the eighteen seventies, was the place where sculpture flourished. All the masters were there, as was a good supply of marble. Artists in other countries made their models from plaster and clay and sent them to Italy to be carved by crews of skilled men. There was no better place at this time to study marble carving. In Italy, Andrew Sr spent much of his time sketching from antique statues. He visited the studios of other artists in his free time and worked from live models in drawing classes, modeling nude figures as well. He was acquiring a good knowledge of anatomy. To most sculptors, making the clay model was considered the creative part of sculpture. Once finished, most of them did not see their work again for months, as it was being enlarged and finished in Italy. After the clay model had received the finishing touches, studio assistants produced a plaster mold, the cast from which, the plaster model was made.

Clay sometimes lost its form if it became too wet or dry, therefore it was important that the piece be put into plaster quickly. The original clay model was destroyed in the process of making the plaster mold. For a portrait bust, workmen in one section of the studio would convert it to marble by a system known as pointing. The pointing machine would measure the depth from a given vertical of the plaster cast and transfer the measurements to a hole drilled in the marble block. Scores of measured depths were transferred this way onto the marble until all that was left for the sculptor was to cut away the surplus stone. For a larger work, the plaster model would be shipped to Carrara, Italy where Italian workmen would block out and finish the statue. O'Connor thoroughly absorbed the procedures required for cutting and carving marble. He had attained the knowledge he craved.

When Andrew Sr. returned from Italy in 1879, he found a job as foreman at 131 Central Street. For the first time in 1880, he was able to be listed in the business section of the Worcester City Directory - as a sculptor.

Once again, Andrew Sr. changed jobs. This time he moved to Lowell, Massachusetts. After all his time pursuing an education, he was dissatisfied to be merely cutting stone. With a growing family his need for more money became greater. Young Andrew was six years old and just starting school, while his brother Charles was three and his sister Adeline, two.

Three years later the O'Connors moved back to Worcester, where the elder found work as a marble cutter at the Boston Marble and Granite Company on 53 Exchange Street with a home address on Christy Street. This pattern of moving from place to place became normal for the O'Connor children, but very difficult for Mary Ella, who was probably promised that someday they would have a permanent home somewhere.

In 1883, nine year old Andrew Jr. was enrolled at the recently constructed Freeland Street School where he made lasting friendships that continued into manhood. As a boy he was very quiet and never indulged in the games and boisterous sports of the other boys. This was undoubtedly a normal reaction for a child who was continually being thrust into new situations.

A love of nature, outdoor life and animals was his escape. He was very interested in canoeing. Whenever he took his boat to the pond, he would take his pet ducks along. Sometimes he fastened strings around the necks of the ducks to keep them from getting too far away from him, prompting members of his family to accuse him of cruelty. This wasn't the case, however. Andrew was interested in studying the motion of the ducks as they swam. He was a great student of form and his love of art made him take advantage of any opportunity that would improve his knowledge of motion.

A taste for drawing developed early. All through the grades at Freeland Street School he was held up as a model to the classes that followed. He didn't show any desire to model clay at that time, but confined himself to drawing. As he grew older he began attending evening drawing classes. From then on, his proficiency was obvious. His instructors recognized that he possessed an extraordinary ability which needed only technical development to flourish, and they joined his father in encouraging him to draw and sketch.

How excited the family must have been, when in 1886, after fourteen years of hard work, O'Connor Sr. was able to open his own business at 98 Front Street in Worcester. The new studio was located in the center of the city in close proximity to City Hall and the 'City Fathers'. It wasn't long before he was approached by the city councilors who asked him to draw plans for a monument to be raised in their new 'Lake Park'. The proposed park was a high rocky hill covered with pine trees, wild juniper and ferns, extending down to Lake Quinsigamond, a seven mile long body of water located east of the City.

Edward L. Davis and Horace Bigelow, both prominent citizens had donated the land to the city. They informed the park commissioners that it was historic ground due to the fact that Indians had kidnapped a boy belonging to the Leonard family at that spot. Horace Bigelow, who loved the land, thought that the city should at least supply the money for a monument to be erected there, commemorating that early chapter of Worcester's Indian history. He felt that this would also be an attraction to the proposed park and draw people to it. When Bigelow suggested that O'Connor Sr. draw the plans for the memorial, he immediately drew a sketch of a statue for the site. The proposed monument would be of colossal size (15 feet) with a base made from the natural boulders and outcroppings of ledge that abounded on the property.

On January 10, 1887 O'Connor Sr. took his drawings to a meeting called by the commissioners where he explained his plan to them. His drawings were of a male figure dressed as a Puritan with a high black hat, waist coat with a wide collar, pants buckled at the knee, hose on the bottom part of the legs and shoes with buckles.

Time passed and O'Connor Sr. did not hear about the commission. When he approached Commissioner Lincoln it was decided that he should do it, but that an independent contractor should do the base. O'Connor agreed, hoping that he could finally begin.

Later that year, Lincoln, the chairman of the commissioners, showed O'Connor Sr. a picture of the new stone tower recently erected in Newport, Rhode Island. He felt that the Puritan, combined with a similar tower would be a good idea. O'Connor agreed even though it meant he would have to make some changes in his model. He then began to design a tower that would provide the statue with a proper base. With the commission for the Puritan a certainty, O'Connor Sr. decided that he needed much more room than he had in his small Front Street studio. He purchased a small building south of the city on 60 Webster Street. The building wasn't large, but the grounds around it were of a size that would accommodate the huge slabs of Connecticut sandstone that he would be using.

On October 24, Commissioner Lincoln decided that all the loose stones around the site were to be taken to the top of the hill to build the tower. He told O'Connor that it could be built by one of the regular park laborers who was "somewhat of a mason".

The foundation was built by the park workers in January of 1888, but nothing was said about the statue till June when the commissioners visited the studio once again and looked at the plans for the statue. When O'Connor Sr. told them that the statue needed to be supported on solid masonry, they decided that it could be "located on a permanent boulder", the suggestion that he had made two years earlier.

Between the other jobs that provided living expenses, O'Connor continued working on the Puritan until June of 1889 when he met with the commissioners once again at Lake Park. They wanted him to check another site rather than the one on the top of the hill where the tower had been built. At this meeting the commission was not willing to furnish the pedestal, but would dig a hole, fill it with rock and cover them with concrete. O'Connor was getting tired of the whole affair.

When Horace Bigelow spoke with some members of the commission he became discouraged with their obstinance about a subject as trivial as a proper pedestal. This was the first time that O'Connor Sr. had become involved in politics and municipal commissioners, and his frustration with the situation was keenly observed by his fourteen year old son, Andrew, and probably remembered well in later years.

1888 proved to be a very upsetting and sad time for O'Connor Sr. Not only were there no decisions made in regard to his *Puritan,* but his home life became severely disrupted. On March 30, 1888, his wife and love of his life, Mary Ella, took ill and passed away. The void left in the family must have been devastating. At fourteen, Andrew was at a particularly difficult age to understand the loss of a parent, while his father not only had to provide a living for the family, but also washed, cleaned and cooked for his young children.

Mary Ella left two sons and three daughters, all suffering from the loss and none understanding why they deserved this or what would now be their fate without a mother to care for and nurture them. It left a frightening fear of death that would never leave Andrew Jr. Young Andrew was old enough to walk to the small studio on Webster Street to spend time with his father. He watched him at work and learned the joy of creating in stone, clay and marble. With his father's instructions he began carving an Indian maiden in marble. Weathering the loss of Mary Ella together forged a strong bond between father and son that remained throughout Andrew Jr.'s life.

The Puritan was finished in 1889 and delivered to Lake Park where it then became the property of the Worcester park department. The bureaucrats stalled year after year, never building a pedestal to support O'Connor's fine tribute to the early American settlers. Over the years, vandals and the weather conspired to separate the top half from the bottom as it lay at the top of Lake Park Hill next to the stone tower, the bronze bas-reliefs on the ground next to it. O'Connor Sr. was destined never to see his Puritan stand.

After the death of his wife, O'Connor began to approach his work in a more business-like manner in order to keep afloat. He published advertisements in the local papers and put out a flyer listing his work.

He not only advertised his portrait sculptures, but also medallion heads. These were made in a plastic substance which gradually hardened and strengthened. The medallions in this plastic material were two inches in diameter and cost twenty five dollars. If they were reproduced in fine white marble, he charged an additional seventy five dollars. Life size busts in the cheaper material were one hundred twenty five dollars and when reproduced in marble or bronze were five hundred dollars extra.

O'Connor's ideas on sculpture were also set forth in his flyer. "Photographs and paintings, as time goes on, assume an appearance known as old fashioned, but humanity is never old fashioned and on this account, sculpture ignores the accompaniments of time and place, and strives to accomplish that which it deems most worthy of effort - preservation of the image of God and the effect upon it of the mind within..

"A popular error concerning the mission of sculpture is to the effect that only those who have done things pleasing to the public mind are worthy of immortality by its means. History teaches the fallacy of this, for as truth advances, these productions are revealed as idols whose claims to continued existence rest not upon what they stood for, but solely upon the humanity stamped upon them."

His flyer stated further: "The glory of a man consists in the fact that he is a distinct creation, an individual without a counterpart in all the universe. The development of this personality is his mission; if he does well his face will show it and if he does ill no art can hide it; in either case, the preservation of it for others is a service to them which the various museums of the world prove they abundantly appreciate." On his flyer O'Connor listed many of the works that he had done for private customers up until this time.

In 1891 O'Connor Sr. was forced to get additional work once again. He became employed as a foreman at a marble cutting business on East Worcester Street and moved his family once again. He still kept his studio open on Webster Street, and a year later left the second job and began working thereafter for himself. Two of the children were in their teens and more able to help with household chores so life was easier, now, but he was lonely without a wife.

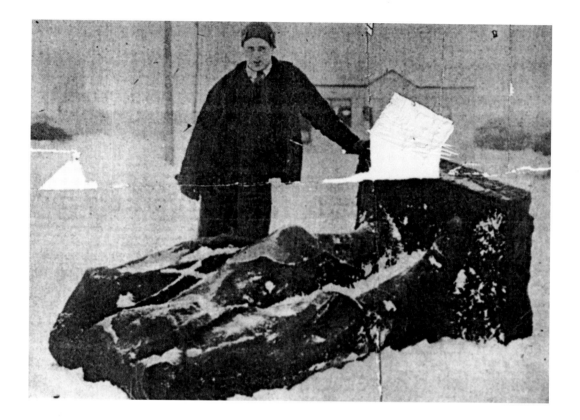

Pictured above "The Puritan" forty years after it had been delivered to the site on Lake Park Hill. Vandals had broken it in half and stolen the head.

II

Chicago

One of Andrew Jr.'s earliest friends in the business of sculpture was young William Ordway Partridge. He was interested in finding work at the Columbian Exposition and pressured Andrew to go to Chicago with him. During 1889 and 1890 the newspapers carried stories about the World's Fair planned to commemorate the four hundredth anniversary of the voyage of Columbus. As time went on, news came out of Chicago that sculptors and architects were needed to build the Fair. Partridge had trained in Europe and was to make his debut as a sculptor at the Exposition.

Andrew talked it over with his father and they decided that the experience would be invaluable. At eighteen years of age the decision to go must have been an exciting one for the boy but a worrisome one for the parent. They had been a source of strength for each other since the loss of Mary Ella and now each had to go it alone. The father knew that his first born son was about to leave the nest permanently - not an easy fact to face. On the fifteen hour train trip from Massachusetts to Illinois Andrew undoubtedly had moments of homesickness for his father and four siblings, as well as sad thoughts of his mother who had so recently died.. It was his first time away from the protection of the familly, and he was still, after all, only a boy.

In 1872 Chicago had suffered a great fire that demolished a large part of the city. The citizens had pulled themselves up by the bootstraps and by 1890 they were ready to tackle the gigantic task of a world's fair. The exposition was to be a great "White City." At first the task seemed almost insurmountable. The site that was chosen was made up of barren sand dunes, surrounded by swamp which abounded with shallow, stagnant, weedy creeks. Even after they had drained the area, the horses that were used to haul material, sank up to their bellies in the spongy surface and temporary planks had to be set down to make a causeway across much of the park.

Vehicles used the plankways to build permanent roads; foundations for the white structures, canals for pleasure boats and standing room for countless feet. Even the soil for the landscaping had to be brought from a distance and progress was made inch by inch and foot by foot. It was a good thing the builders did not know in advance how great the job would be. They would have recoiled at the mere thought.

Imagine... it is five o'clock on Saturday afternoon. From the upper gateway of the park pours a stream of workmen and visitors returning to the city... whose edges are not far away, but whose buisness center is miles away. Here is a good spot from which to view the artisans whose hands are building the World's Fair. Italian staff workers and sculptor's assistants are there in force. There are Germans and Scandinavians, Frenchmen and Poles, Bohemians and Russians, Spaniards and Greeks, white men and black; thousands! They are pouring out in a deluge that will inundate the approaches to the grounds until the railway trains and cable cars draw them off during the sixty minutes that will pass before the second inundation or workers who will be free to go home at six o'clock. With all this help, the Fair had to be ready on time.

Although there were many languages spoken by this multitude of homeward bound workers, the roar of Anglo-Saxon dominated, for notwithstanding the huge number of foreign speaking persons, the Americans were building the World's Fair. They came from everywhere: the Westerners who were never daunted by any task given them, the New Englanders, who were the sculptors and their assistants; the mechanics from the middle states, and some from the southern states. These joined with the Chicagoans, the wood carvers from Switzerland and the Italian staff moulders that made up the cosmopolitan group all working to finish the buildings on time. Chicago in the winter of 1892-1893 was host to a gathering of artists that, as the famous sculptor Augustus St. Gaudens exclaimed "had not been assembled since the great days of the Renaissance." What an exciting experience for an eighteen year old neophyte.

It had been decided in the planning phase of the fair, that all the buildings surrounding the large central lagoon, would be white. Louis Sullivan, a leading Chicago architect, was not happy with this idea, so his building alone would be colored differently.

The well known and capable sculptor Daniel Chester French was assigned the colossal figure representing the *Republic* which was to tower sixty five feet above the lagoon. At the opposite end was Frederic MacMonnies *Triumphant Barge of State* in the company of splashing dolphins and tritons.

The colossal scale of the great White City required that the figure of the *Republic* be enormous if it were truly to be a focal point of the lagoon and also work well with the twelve palaces and the triumphal arch that were to surround the great basin. French had made his models of the *Republic*. Now he needed assistants to help with the enlarging process and all of the mixing and applying of the base material to cover the forms. Consequently, he interviewed O'Connor, who showed him the small marble of an Indian maiden he had carved. French was impressed with his work and hired him immediately, along with young Henry Augustus Lukeman. They were to work in the large Forestry Building that was being used as a temporary studio. Andrew was extremely interested in the mechanics of making a huge statue from the small model that French had designed.

12.

A gigantic wooden frame was soon built, over which the staff mixture of plaster and straw was pressed into every space. The figure of the woman who represented the *Republic* was then covered with gold leaf everywhere but the head and arms. Clothed in a full length robe with ample folds, the *Republic* had a classic majesty that worked well with the neo-Renaissance architecture that surrounded the lagoon. Most impressive was the wreath around her head containing an awesome display of electric lights, an innovation in 1893.

It was a grandiose spectacle, but like all the decorations made of staff, it wouldn't last long after the closing of the fair. A smaller gilded bronze replica was produced in 1916 and may still be seen in Chicago.

Andrew was working very hard, meeting many important people in the art world and becoming good friends with a few, one of whom was Louis Sullivan, the great architect from Chicago who built the first sky scraper.

Working on the preparations for the fair was no bed of roses. The winter of 1892-1893 was severe with its extreme cold, heavy snowfall and terrible blizzards. By gigantic efforts the buildings were roofed before the first storms and through the long winter they proved to be well built. There were problems with those buildings that had large expanses of glass. The weight of the snow collapsed roofs, especially when it fell from a higher roof to one below. The actual money damages were not great, but there were exhibitors who were reluctant to bring work into their exhibit areas too early, for fear of loss or injury to it. Still, an enormous amount of articles arrived daily. They were brought onto the fair grounds and into the buildings themselves by railway trains whose network connected to the general railway system of the city.

The miserable winter was finally over, Spring was slow in coming, and the supervisors in charge of setting everything in place and in running condition began to panic. All work-outside and indoors, was going on at the same time. With railroad tracks everywhere, it was impossible to build or asphalt roads. There were so many people filling the area with their loading and unloading that the road builders were becoming more and more frustrated. Everyone who worked in Jackson Park, Chicago in March and April of 1893 looked back on it as some kind of nightmare.

More than once the Directory announced a date when the inner railway tracks had to be removed, and just as often the day was postponed to give exhibitors time to get in their goods, wares and machinery that could not be delivered except by rail. When the tracks were finally torn up and the huge engines rolled out, time was too short to build quality roadways. The avenues leading to all the gates were in very poor condition. Carriages and horses were dripping with mud by the time they arrived on the grounds, and loaded teams were stuck in the mud everywhere.

The statuary, bas-reliefs and exteriors of all the buildings that had been faced with the *staff* mixture had withstood the winter's freezing and thawing very well, however they were dirty and stained. To restore the White City it was necessary to spray everything with a liquid coloring by forcing compressed air through a hose much as fire engines throw water on a fire.

The Fair dealt with the present and future except for exhibits that described Columbus. One building that made a lasting impression on Andrew was the ancient Spanish building known as the convent of Santa Maria La Rabida, (Saint Mary of the Frontier). Dating back to Roman times, it was the temple to Proserpina. The Christians made a convent of it, the Moors drove them out and made it a Mohammedan mosque. Then the Knights Templar held it for centuries as a Chapter House, and in the twelfth century its original character was restored and maintained. It remained as a Chapter House up to and including Columbus' time. During the Columbian renaissance, the Spanish government re-established it and in 1892 the Queen Regent placed the Franciscan order again in permanent possession. The building in Chicago was an exact copy of the original convent. Enormous doors, corridors, galleries, passages and verandas, its prison-like cells and miniature chapel were crowded almost to bursting day after day. Millions went through it in the course of the fair, which was an enormous success.

The original convent overlooks the harbor of Palos, Spain, the port from which Columbus set sail on his voyage. It had been his shelter years before at the time of his direst need, and it was here that he made the acquaintance of the prior of the convent, Jaun Perez, a friend who stuck with him through all his trials. Without the help of the prior, he never would have been noticed by Queen Isabella.

The reproduced convent was faultless in its construction and surroundings. It stood on a low promontory of rock built into the lake, surrounded on three sides by water. The walls rose grey and grim and the small windows looked out on the sunrise, sky and water. It was completely different from any other structure at the Fair.

The contents of La Rabida were priceless. The Spanish Government and descendants of Columbus loaned the original contract with Ferdinand and Isabella for his first voyage. Also on loan were his commission as Admiral of the Ocean Seas, his correspondence with them before and after his discoveries, and many other interesting artifacts. Andrew loved everything about La Rabida an visited it time and again. It was so unlike anything he had known in his short life.

Eighty different portraits of Columbus were displayed on the walls of the rooms, all alleging to be true likenesses and each having experts attest to their authenticity, but none looking like another. In fact, no one could have identified them as the same man.

The Columbian Exposition was a great learning experience for Andrew O'Connor Jr. Finally in May of 1893, the gates to the Fair were opened to the public. Andrew's work in Chicago was finished and he went home to Worcester. To be reunited with his family and relate all of the exciting experiences he had enjoyed in the past two years was heartwarming and joyful. His father had written to him about his own happiness. When Andrew left, Sr. had married a young woman named Cora Paige. She, in due time, delivered twins, Mildred and Harrison. The baby boy died when he was a year old, leaving little Mildred an only child. She proved to be a welcome addition to the

Judge Henry Chapin,
Founder of Worcester State College.
Bust located at College,
Worcester, Massachusetts.

family, for the older children were leaving the fold one by one. O'Connor Sr. was very busy on cemetery monuments and marble busts of Worcester's luminaries.

Three busts that were done at this time are accessible today, a hundred years later, in the city. One very important man to the city of Worcester was Judge Henry Chapin, influential in establishing the State Normal School, now called Worcester State College. He also worked to establish the Worcester Insane Asylum, later named Worcester State Hospital known for many years as one of the finest mental institutions in the country. His bust is now located in Worcester State College. The second was a portrait bust of Willie Grout, the first soldier from Worcester to be killed in the Civil War. This was placed in Commerce High School, was later moved to the Historical Museum when the school was no longer in use.

A Jesuit priest who had been named the first bishop of Springfield, Massachusetts during the years of 1870-1892, also sat for a portrait bust by O'Connor Sr. The bust of Father Thomas O'Reilly is located at Holy Cross College Library in Worcester.

In the Spring of 1894 Daniel Chester French, who had hired O'Connor and Henry Gustave Lukeman in Chicago, found his business growing by leaps and bounds. Soon he had work ahead for the next ten years, and a waiting list for new commissions. Lukeman and O'Connnor had done such a fine job for him in Chicago that he contacted them to help him in New York City where French owned a studio on Eighth street. Upstairs in the building there were rooms provided for his employees, and Andrew moved in immediately. The studio was conveniently located two blocks from French's residence on Tenth street, making it a pleasant walk to his work. When Andrew began working for French, one of the works in progress was a set of doors for the Boston Public Library which the architectural firm of McKim, Mead and White was designing. Andrew had no idea how doors were crafted, so it was with great interest and enthusiasm that he began learning the process from French.

Daniel Chester French was born in Exeter, New Hampshire April 20, 1850. He was the youngest of four children of Anne

Richardson of Cambridge, Massachusetts and Henry French who practiced law in Boston. In the Fall of 1867 when the family was living in Concord, young French, at the urging of his father, enrolled in the Massachusetts Institute of Technology. He was not happy there and left after a short while. He had always been interested in modelling figures and decided he would be happier studying sculpture. His father agreed, and suggested that he should go to Europe for the proper training.

When he reached Paris, his friends advised him to go on to Florence, Italy and study there. French remained in Italy for approximately eighteen months and then went on to study with William Rimmer for two winters, where he learned the production of a work of sculpture.

French was a modeler, not a carver, and preferred to work in water-soluble clay. Later on, as plasteline, an oil based clay became available, he worked with that. He also used wax for modelling miniatures. His portrait busts of the 1880's were sculpted in clay, transferred to plaster and the task of translating the plaster sculpture into marble or other stone was performed by trained Italian craftsmen. He once explained his preference in craftsmen to two of his clients; "Having my marble work done in Italy has its inconveniences, but both marble and workmanship are far superior to what I could get here." Andrew had been accustomed to watching his father, who sculpted his figures full size, in marble or other stone. Between chores, he learned by

Willie Grout, first soldier from Worcester killed in the Civil War. Bust located in the Worcester Historical Museum.

Father Thomas O'Reilly.
Holy Cross Library,
Worcester, Massachusetts.

17.

observing French at work, or helping with carving when needed. An essential duty of studio men was squirting water on the clay statues to keep them from drying out. Steel syringes in buckets of water were kept near the statues for this purpose. The wetting down was a continuous process, for if the clay was allowed to dry, it became hard and brittle. At night the statue was syringed, covered with wet cloths and surrounded by oilcloth screens to keep in the moisture. All the screens had to be removed in the morning before French arrived in the studio. His tools were laid out, the coverings removed, and blocks of clay readied and placed next to the statue to be worked on that day. During the day he lifted, carried and cleaned as needed.

A sculptor could not complete a work of any significance without the help of studio assistants as well as the expertise of an architect who blended the statue and its pedestal with the site. As French once said, "The effect of a monument or statue rightly does a great deal for an establishment or city square. I have come to feel that a mediocre statue, rightly placed is of more value and importance than a good statue badly installed. The important thing is not to find a site for a statue, but a statue for a site."

Daniel Chester French was one of the country's finest sculptors, and also good friends with another, Augustus St. Gaudens, who was almost the same age as he. St. Gaudens, who became known to O'Connor in Chicago, was one of the most famous American masters of the trade He was born in Dublin, Ireland in 1848. His father was French and his mother Irish, thus the French name. He came to the United States as a child, but when he was thirteen his father told him it was time to pick a trade. He chose to be an artist. His father knew of his interest in art because of the sketches he drew everywhere he went, on any blank space, be it a fence or a wall. The senior St. Gaudens arranged for "Gus" to study with a cameo cutter named Avet. The disposition of Avet was difficult and he left, but not until he had acquired a good knowledge of cameo cutting. He went on to execute not only beautiful cameos, but many beautiful statues. He was in a class by himself. At eighteen, St.Gaudens took classes at the National Academy of Design. At nineteen he went to Paris where he took classes at L'Ecole de Medicede. He was one of the first Americans to study at L'Ecole des Beaux Arts in Paris.

It is thought that St. Gaudens and D.C. French met while competing for the commission of a statue in Boston. In the early part of the 1890's French spent three summers at the home and studio of St. Gaudens in Cornish, New Hampshire, in the company of other artists who found inspiration working near each other in the summer months. Called 'Aspet', the house was later enlarged and winterized, making it a year round home.

In 1893 French was busy with the doors for the Boston Library, and he was also working on an equestrian statue of Ulysses Grant. This was a wonderful piece from which O'Connor learned to sculpt the rider of a horse. The horse itself was done by another artisan, as French did not craft horses.

One day a gentleman who introduced himself as John Singer Sargent, came to the studio to speak with French. He had been commissioned to paint some very large murals for the entrance of the Boston Public Library. Charles McKim, a member of the architectural firm of McKim, Mead and White, was designing the new building, and White advised Sargent to speak with French in order that they might correlate the design of the doors with the murals inside.

O'Connor had been working on the doors under the direction of French, so it followed that he would suggest that his young assistant might be helpful to Sargent. Also, since the Grant Equestrian was finished French was eager to be away from New York for the summer. He and his wife liked the idea of St. Gauden's studio in the country and had been looking for one of their own on their summer vacations in New England.

When Sargent had been given the commission for the murals, he immediately took a twenty year lease on a huge studio on numbers twelve and fourteen of the 'Avenue' (76 Fulham Rd.) in London. Since he had ample space, he hired Andrew to come to London and work for him until the murals were completed. He was somewhat nervous about painting anything as large as the murals would be. They were to be placed just inside the entrance to the new library, over the doors and reaching to the ceiling. Sargent was a very accomplished artist by this time in his life, and had the friendship of many Boston people.

Sargent welcomed O'Connor's presence. Not only did Andrew give Sargent moral support and design ideas from the doors that French was carving, he also posed as one of the prophets in the 'Frieze of Prophets'. In his free time Andrew visited museums and studied the work of other artists. No doubt as he worked with Sargent, the conversation turned to the artists whose work each of them admired most.

The brittle and sophisticated society of London did not appeal to Sargent's modest and retiring character, but Andrew went out in his free time and made friends with some of the young struggling local artists. In the studio Andrew listened with interest as Sargent talked about his background. It was so unlike his own younger years. Born in Florence, Italy in 1856 of American parents, Sargent first saw America at the age of twenty when his mother brought him and his sister Emily to the Centennial Exposition in Philadelphia in the summer of 1876. Although they spent four months sight-seeing and visiting their friends, their itinerary did not bring them to Massachusetts where his father's parents lived. Sargent was never able to meet his grandparents.

John Sargent's mother was an only child, but his father came from a large family in Gloucester, Massachusetts. His grandfather had left the family in 1830 and moved to Philadelphia where his father, a successful surgeon, grew up. His father had written several textbooks, retired, and on his wife's urging, moved to Europe. His children were raised in Europe and the family moved constantly. John's mother was restless, and followed the nice weather from one part of the continent to the other.

Mrs. Sargent returned to the United States only once. With her two children, she traveled to Newport, Saratoga, Niagara, Lake George, Quebec and then to Philadelphia. She had forgotten how hot the city was in the summertime, and became so upset with the weather that she went back to Europe, never to return.

John Singer Sargent enjoyed America. He had friends there and felt strongly drawn to his relatives in Gloucester. He especially felt at home in Boston, and the people there recognized his talent and thought of him as theirs. He had his first and second art exhibits in Boston, and his association with many of the city's famous personalities is an important chapter in the cultural history of Boston. Boston people thought of Sargent as an American and Sargent created the Boston of the nineteenth century as Copley had created the colonial city a hundred years before.

It was noted that an increasing grandeur became evident in Sargent's portraiture towards the end of the 1890's. His dissatisfaction with impressionistic qualities of style and the ambitions fostered by his Boston Library murals combined with the need to produce something new. These all affected his developement. Also, as he and O'Connor worked together a new dimension was added to each. In the more than two years that he spent with John Sargent, O'Connor strengthened his skills in sketching and drawing the human figure in groups. He would use this knowledge many times in his career.

In later years Andrew would tell his children the story about a small commission he had in York, England. He was doing some repair work on the outside of a large church there. As he worked, the children in the neighborhood danced around him singing:

> *Andrew from London*
> *Andrew from Cork*
> *With a hole in his britches*
> *As big as New York.*

Although his father continued to write to him often, to encourage and remind him of his good fortune in having such a fine opportunity to learn this part of his trade, there were times that Andrew was lonely in London. He was yearning to return to his own family and country. By 1897, when Sargent had a commission outside of London and his need for O'Connor's services was over, Andrew was relieved to be going home. When he returned to New York, young O'Connor made his way directly to French's studio to make certain he still had work there as a studio assistant. He was given the same living quarters in the room on the top floor of French's building appreciating the fact that it was very convenient and economical.

Andrew wasn't home long before he became friends with a young model named Nora. They began going out after working hours sometimes to the local pub that the young artists of the area frequented, sometimes for a walk and occasionally back to his or her room. It wasn't long before the young lady became pregnant, and there was no alternative in Andrew's mind but he must marry her. In this relationship there was no question of love, only companionship between two lonely people.

Since apartments and tenements were priced exorbitantly high in Manhattan, they were forced to find something within their means, and were soon ensconced in their own small place in Brooklyn. Money was very tight, but Andrew worked harder than ever and French began to steer work his way. In due time, a new addition to the small family arrived in the form of a beautiful little girl name 'Aster'.

The elder O'Connor was finally making enough money to purchase a home for Cora and Mildred. They found a house in the suburbs of Worcester, in a small town called Holden. The house had a garage behind it that O'Connor Sr. quickly set up as his studio. There was enough land with it to accommodate his large slabs of stone as well.

In 1898 Andrew Sr. was approached for a new commission. The survivors and friends of the 15th. Massachusetts regiment who had fought in the battle of Sharpsburg, Maryland in the Civil War were interested in erecting a monument at the cemetery at Antietam. This would be a welcome change from cemetery stones and portrait busts. His design was of a wounded lion to be carved from granite. Approximately ten feet long and three feet high at the head, the lion was to typify the regiment's stubborn resistance when out-flanked, and forced from the field.

The battle of Antietam (or Sharpsburg) on September 17, 1862, climaxed the first of Confederate Gen. Robert E. Lee's two attempts to carry the war into the North. About 40,000 Southeners were pitted against the 87,000 man Federal Army of the Potomac under Gen. George B. McClennan. When the fighting ended, the course of the American Civil War had been greatly altered.

The Wounded Lion.
Sculpted by Andrew O'Connor Sr.
Located on Hagerstown Pike and
Cornfield Avenue in Antietam National
Cemetery, Sharpsburg, M.D.

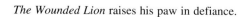

The Wounded Lion raises his paw in defiance.

III

New York and D.C. French

French and his wife had been busy in Andrew's absence. They had purchased a farm near Stockbridge, Mass. Consequently, they would be working closer to Worcester and Andrew's home, at least in the summertime. French had named his summer studio Chesterwood.

He had once remarked to a newspaper reporter, "I spend six months of the year up there. That is heaven; New York is - well, New York." Beginning in 1897, French left his home in New York City when summer came and moved his studio to the Berkshire Hills of western Massachusetts.

There was a large barn behind the main house and up a small grade. Next to the house was his studio. He was always within earshot of the activities in the house.

French was very excited about the old farm and impatient to get started on making it his summer estate. The main building was old, needing many repairs. Once renovated however, paint, wallpaper and furniture finished the home beautifully. Wicker furniture for the front porch that faced the Housatonic River and Monument Mountain, was the final touch.

As a barn is the most important building to a farmer, the studio was the most important building to a sculptor. An architect friend of D.C. French, Henry Bacon, designed it to his specifications and everything he ever wanted in a studio was incorporated into this one. The main room was thirty feet by twenty nine feet, the ceiling height twenty three feet with a hip roof of fifteen feet. The height was very important for large commissions. A must for every artist was the skylight on the north side for overhead lighting, and plenty of windows for side lighting.

After working with the railroad track that came right into the building at the Chicago exposition, he wanted that convenience in his own studio. Joined to a turntable it went through the large doors to the outside. French was most emphatic that a statue should be viewed in outside light where it would ultimately stand.

The set of trap doors in the studio, convenient to the casting room, was a work saver for Andrew. Through these trap doors in the floor, any object not in use, was easily passed into the basement and best of all, the plaster clay and mess from the day's work could be swept through this opening into a chute which led to a barrel below. There was step ladder on wheels convenient for reaching the higher parts of large statues. There were also stands on wheels to accommodate small pieces that could be wheeled out of the way when not in progress.

Andrew Jr. enjoyed working for Daniel Chester French. The Boston Public Library doors were still in the process of being completed, so he spent much of his time working on them, to the degree that he became very adept at carving doors. He also learned the business side of the art as clients came to view whatever was in progress, and sometimes to disagree with the way the work was going. They would sometimes request that a figure be changed and depending on how difficult it would be, the changes might be made. Part of what he learned was that the artist had to sign contracts, pay his assistants, purchase insurance and buy materials to do the monument, all before he was given any money at all. After reasonable progress had been made, the client would release a part of the money due, but not until the statue was ready for unveiling did the sculptor receive the agreed amount that the contract stipulated. The artist had to have ready funds in order to begin a statue at all. This part of the business was always difficult for O'Connor to manage.

French often said that he much preferred working for a single client than a commission. Once he frustratedly commented that "the committee is the worst foe to monumental work that exists".

An important person in the life of D.C. French and later on - O'Connor, was Stanford White, the architect. White was a business associate of French's, who sent commissions his way and when French needed a pedestal for his monuments, White reciprocated. They were both prominent in New York society and saw each other frequently when they were enjoying their free evenings..

White was from a middle class family and was an extremely gifted artist. He had apprenticed under the famous architect H.B Richardson at the age of sixteen. At age twenty-five he started his own business, joining with McKim and Mead to form the firm of McKim, Mead and White.

White was married to a very wealthy woman and they had one child. Though he surely loved her, when she went off to the country every summer to be away from New York, 'Stanny', as his friends called him, socialized wherever there was any activity going on that involved good times and people, especially women. He had a wonderful personality and everyone who knew him, liked him enormously. There were many people who were indebted to him for the help he gave them in getting started in their careers. The firm of McKim, Mead, and White had commissions all over the Northeast United States. They built mansions, banks, businesses and churches in New York City, as well as the beautiful summer "cottages" in Newport, Rhode Island. Not only did White design the "cottages," but he was a talented interior decorator and finished them as well.

In 1899, White was approached by Alice Gwynne Vanderbilt, who asked him to design new doors for the St.Bartholomew Church, located at the southwest corner of Madison Avenue and 44th. Street in New York. She wanted to donate the bronze doors in memory of her late husband, Cornelius. In his inimitable fashion, White convinced her that the doors would look much nicer on a new porch that could be added to the front of the building. Since money was no object, she agreed, and White asked French to design and craft the doors. French knew how well Andrew was doing on the Boston Library doors, and he had more work than he could handle, therefore he suggested that O'Connor was capable of doing them. White agreed that they should give the boy a chance, and French said he would keep his eye on the project to ensure that it was done properly. He also agreed to carve the tympanum, or arched space above the central doorway, with the assistance of O'Connor.

Corinthian columns of Cippolino marble framed the three portals of Indiana limestone and supported the frieze with Biblical scenes flanking the central entrance. O'Connor carved the frieze and decorated the central doorway with cast bronze panels illustrating the lives of the Apostles.

The completion of the beautiful bronze doors was O'Connor's debut into the professional art arena. Everyone who knew fine work was very excited about the results. St. Gaudens paid a special visit to the studio to congratulate him. He thought that White too, had outdone himself on the porch design, and that the church as a whole was "really bully, and that's saying a good deal, old man."

The publicity gave O'Connor overnight fame. Mrs. Vanderbilt, the donor, was very much pleased with the work, and "confident that it will mark an era in American art." About the same time as the St. Bartholomew addition, Stanford White was designing another building on Fifth Avenue. The Gorham Silver Company wanted a new showcase for the display of the many products they sold. They also wanted a workshop where their goods could be made. O'Connor was to embellish the front entrance, a colonnade with polished gray granite columns on either side and the spaces above the arches.

Center Doors and Porch of St. Bartholomew's Church.
Doors crafted by O'Connor Jr. and work above the
28. doors by D.C. French and O'Connor
    Church location; 109 E. 50th. ST. New York, N.Y.

White stated at the finish of the job that; "O'Connor, who did such splendid work on St. Bartholomew's Church, has created a series of allegorical figures of art and industry relating to the silversmith's trade." White had his eye on all parts of the construction of his buildings and was very satisfied with O'Connor's work.

As he began to get more commissions, O'Connor's name became more familiar to the art world, and he was accumulating a little money - a new experience for him.

At home in Brooklyn, everything centered around Aster, the new baby and Andrew found life hectic. He was not at an age when babies were of interest to him, and all of the new work he was getting became far more time consuming and thought provoking. He commuted daily to the city and of necessity stayed there till late at night, coming home only to sleep and be off again early in the morning.

With so many new commissions Andrew leased space on MacDougal Alley near French's studio, a convenient arrangement. When he was needed, he worked for French, otherwise, he found it exhilarating to be in his own place. In 1902, Andrew hired a model, Jesse Phoebe Brown. She was a beautiful, auburn haired young woman. Shy, composed and Junoesque, she was lovely. Andrew was intrigued with the fact that at twenty six, she was a virgin, something that was unheard of at her age. By the standards of the time, she was fast becoming an old maid.

There were two kinds of artist models at this time, those who removed their clothes and those who preferred not to pose nude. Jesse was the latter, always wearing a costume of some sort. Andrew looked forward to the days when Jesse would be working, never tiring of looking at her lovely face and figure. She was very shy, but that suited O'Connor, for he loved to talk and was flattered that she listened attentively. Work assumed a new dimension for Andrew with Jesse there, and Brooklyn and its responsibilities began to fade from the forefront of his priorities. Andrew was in love for the first time in his life.

Late that year O'Connor completed a memorial to Emerson Liscum to be placed in Arlington National Cemetery. It stands on a hill in the older section. A bust of the same design was later sold to the Metropolitan Museum in New York titled *Le Gloire Militaire.*

Several statues of Virgins dated from this time when Jesse first began working for O'Connor Jr.. She also modeled for the crowning figure in the pediment of the Art Palace at the St. Louis Exposition of 1904. Again, she modeled for the figure on the door of the Loney Family Tomb in Skaneateles, New York. The architect, Cass Gilbert, had offered the Loney commission to French, whose work load continued to be so great, he turned the job over to O'Connor. He always wanted to help Andrew and now he thought that his pupil should fly on his own.

A series of commissions followed. The doors of the Miner's Bank in Pottsville, Pennsylvania contained six strong figures of workers. The common man often became a subject of O'Connor's craft. Having an Irish working class background made him vitally aware of the problems of the working class. In the relative confinement of the form and media of doors, O'Connor managed to capture the strength and motion of the laborers. He did this by varying the positions and occupations of the men and although each worker was different in his facial expressions as well as body position, the door does not appear to be disorganized, but almost perfectly symmetrical. In the lion ring door handles, the lion's manes are curled so that they blend with the sunburst higher on the doors and the lion itself becomes a symbol of the strength of the laborers.

Also at this time, O'Connor Jr. executed the bronze doors for the Temple Emanuel on Fifth Avenue in New York City. The basic order is evident with rectangular outlines and four pair or flowered medallions. On these doors he used the same devices to destroy order and symmetry as he did to create it on the Miner's Bank doors. The effect is interesting and definitely reflects the Eastern culture. Once it became known in the art world that O'Connor was sculpting beautiful doors, everyone who needed them thought of him. D.C. French, Stanford White and Cass Gilbert gave him all the work he could handle and he was literally working from early morning to nine at night.

Miner's Bank Doors. Pottsville, Pennsylvania.

31.

Truth, posed by Jesse Phoebe Brown.

Power, posed by Andrew Sr.

A different design makes up the American Insurance Company doors of Newark, New Jersey. Once again O'Connor Jr. uses the human figure, a winged male on the right and a female on the left. These doors were given to the Newark Museum of Art in 1980 by the Public Service Electric and Gas company who owned the building at that time. They are now installed in the renovated south wing of the Museum.

Along with the cornice and parapet of the front entrance to the Pierpont Morgan Library on 29 East 36th. Street in New York City, O'Connor sculpted the lunette above the doors. He also did the two 'putti' supporting the logo of Aldus Manutius, the great Renaissance printer and scholar. All of these works were completed while O'Connor was under the guidance of D.C. French.

Cass Gilbert was designing some fine buildings in the early 1900's, among them, the New York Custom House in lower Manhattan. This building is located at the foot of Broadway, immediately south of Bowling Green. Four large statues representing the Continents of Europe, Asia, Africa and America were placed in front of the building. One group stands at each front corner, and two flank the entrance. French expected O'Connor to help with the groups representing the Continents and as an incentive, gave him the job of carving the area above the main entrance. Gilbert was so happy with O'Connor's *Columbia* that presides over the Custom House entrance, he commissioned him to design and execute a series of statues for the Essex County Courthouse in Newark, New Jersey.

Cass Gilbert's courthouse sits on a small hill facing the city of Newark. A long flight of stairs, the width of the building, leads to the front entrance. On either side of the stairs is a seated figure. On the left in bronze is a woman representing *Truth*, posed by Jesse, and on the right, a figure representing *Power*, posed by Andrew Sr. Each figure has bronze bas-reliefs in the pedestal with figures representing features of the law. Across the cornice of the building from left to right are the statues of *Light, Reason, Law, Maternity*, or shelter of law; *Thais*, or protection of law; *Cain*, or assault of law; and *Learning*, or authority of law. On the apex of the roof was *Power* of law, or *Mars*.

The statue of *Power* was also called *Justice.* Andrew was delighted when his father finally came to New York to visit him and see his new studio. He prevailed upon him to pose for the statue of *Power* while he was there, giving them time to be together and enjoy each others company.

After completing the Essex County Courthouse statues, O'Connor began work on a memorial figure for the Thomas family of Tarrytown, New York. This was in memory of General Samuel Thomas, to be placed in front of his burial vault in Sleepy Hollow Cemetary. Mrs. Thomas wanted it to be a "sort of meditation." Jesse Phoebe Brown posed for it in a seated position with her head bowed slightly. O'Connor named it *Recuillement,* or *Grief.* He was very pleased with the statue on its completion, but when Mrs. Thomas came to the studio for the final viewing, she was disappointed that the figure was not gay and smiling. O'Connor advised her to come back a week later and he would show her another head.

The following week Mrs. Thomas returned and was shown another head that had something more frivolous about it and she was delighted. As she pulled out her checkbook she said, "Knock the other head off and put this one on." O'Connor let the new head fall to the floor where it smashed. "I just made this to show you that I could do it," he said politely, "but I should never let such a monstrosity out of my studio." The monument was accepted and installed next to the mausoleum in which General Thomas rests.

Statues representing different aspects of the law. Essex County Courthouse Rooftop.

Recuillement.
See page 117.

O'Connor used the *Recuillement* mold for several other statues. He sold a portrait bust of it for the pedestal of another cemetery memorial carved in Vermont granite. Another smaller version of the head and neck only was done in bronze, and a full seated version of the statue carved in Connecticut limestone is in Balboa Park, San Diego, California. Although the statue in Tarrytown has been streaked by time and weather, it is so life-like that one feels the urge to touch the hands of Jesse that are folded one upon the other at the knee. It is said that school children who come to this incredibly beautiful cemetery to view the monuments located there, invariably hurry to the small hill where Jesse sits in fair weather or foul.

Jesse was now Andrew's only model. She had long ago fallen in love with the tall, dark, handsome sculptor. She was young, beautiful, and always at hand, ready to model anything that required a human figure. O'Connor, in his turn, obviously found Jesse enchanting, and never tired of taking casts of her face to be set aside for future use. A love began to grow on his part, and at the same time, Jesse realized how easy it was for a model to entice the artist. She began to get territorial, and insisted that she could model for all of his work, male or female.

What eventually was to become an extremely important commmission for O'Connor Jr. was a statue to the memory of General Henry Lawton of Indianapolis, Indiana. General Lawton had enlisted in the infantry at the beginning of the Civil War and rose to become a Lieuetenant Colonel. After he was mustered out, he went back to college for a while, but enlisted in the infantry again to fight the Indian wars. He fought again in the infantry in the Spanish-American War and rose to become a Brigadier General. After returning to the United States, he accompanied President Theodore Roosevelt on one of his tours of the country, after which he took command of the Army Corps at Huntsville, Alabama. Ordered to the Philippines in 1889, he reached Manila on March 18, and was placed in command of his First Division, Eighth Army Corps. On December 19, 1889, while getting his troops ready to cross the river to San Mateo, he was shot through the heart. Lawton was a striking figure of six feet four inches, energetic in his actions and a fine field soldier, who was respected and loved by his associates.

The statue was to be paid for with contributions from the people of Indiana. Caught up in the new project, O'Connor began sketching the figure, and getting the materials ready to begin modeling. He was hardly prepared when Jesse brought him the news that she was pregnant! Suddenly Andrew's life went into a tailspin. What should he do? He had just begun to establish himself as a good sculptor, commissions were coming in steadily, and he still had a wife and child in the small apartment in Brooklyn. Although he and Nora were good friends, there was never the love between them that he felt for Jesse. Faced with a dilemma, he tried to think of a way out, but it always came back to the time element. There wasn't much time before the child would be born. He was too ashamed to ask advice from his father, and D.C. French would not want to be involved in such a difficult decision. If he left Nora, he would of course support her financially, but he couldn't bear to let Jesse face the future as an unwed mother. In the early years of the twentieth century, this was scandalous. There wasn't time to work it out. He decided to pack everything and leave New York City with Jesse. His destination, after little thought, would be Paris. Thus Andrew O'Connor changed his whole future in one difficult and rash move.

35.

Brigadier General Henry Lawton.   Garfield Park, Indianapolis, Ind.

IV

Paris and Rodin

When they reached Paris, Andrew rented an atelier at 84 Boulevard Garibaldi and threw himself into the work involved in the General Henry Lawton monument.

During the winter of 1905, Jesse delivered a healthy baby boy that they named Hector. The O'Connors soon adjusted their lives to a baby, learning a new language, and becoming comfortable with their new neighbors in the artist's community that flourished in Paris at that time.

Andrew's life expanded. New doors opened, giving a different meaning to his work. He had long been interested in the sculpture of Auguste Rodin, and began dropping by the Rodin studio, first to meet the artist and later to visit as a friend. Rodin had reached the time in his life when he enjoyed entertaining visitors. He was not producing much, and this new and promising young sculptor from New York was welcome whenever he appeared. Writing to his father, Andrew shared his admiration of the way that Rodin carved his beautiful figures from rough stone. The back and sides of the stone remained untouched, but the figures carved into it, had a satin- like finish. It was not long before O'Connor Sr's gravestones began to have rough backs and sides and the part that bore the inscription was satin smooth. Judging by the number of these monuments in the cemeteries of his city, business must have been prosperous for O'Connor Sr. as well as other stone carvers in 1905 and 1906.

Every year the enormous art community in Paris held an exhibition of their works at the Salon des Beaux Arts. Rodin at this time was very influential in the operation of the Salon, and after seeing the finished General Lawton, advised Andrew to exhibit it in the 1906 Salon. It was a great surprise to everyone when the silver medal was awarded to O'Connor the very first time he exhibited, for there were thousands of artists who put their work in the Salon every spring.

Gold and silver medals were given for the best work of art. The judges were probably the best art critics in the world. O'Connor was proud of the medal, he was the first foreigner to ever be so honored. Later, many said he should have received the Salon's first prize and did not because he was not French. A controversy developed over this, and in the French publication L'Art M.Guillemot, a leading critic wrote; "It is not right to suppress these medals and other baubles dear to the artistic senses.

"It is more than time to put into actual practice our French courtesy by proclaiming all these awards accessible to exhibitors without distinction of nationality - taking into account merely the same spirit toward another stranger who has lately come to establish himself at Paris. I mean Mr. Andrew O'Connor, whose statue is, in my opinion one of the most distinguished works in the last Salon.

"The head firmly and skillfully chiseled, is shaded by the visor rim of the colonial helmet which fits him perfectly. His clothing, boots, and hands are treated in a masterful manner. You feel yourself there in the presence of a sculptor most richly endowed, to whom chicanery and pretense are absolutely unknown."

M. Guillemot happened to be a good friend of Royal Cortissoz, an art critic from New York who knew O'Connor. On one of his visits to Paris, Cortissoz asked Guillemot if he would like to visit the O'Connor studio. This resulted in further editorial comment:

"I had the good fortune to make the acquaintance of the American sculptor, and visit his studio. I have been able to take account of the undeniable superiority of many other of his works of art. For today, I limit myself to adding that if Mr. O'Connor is a foreigner he is certain soon to be adopted as a Parisian by every honest man capable of appreciating the indisputable purity of his character, a purity which will constantly keep him a stranger to the myriad intrigues of our different cliques which are the eyesores of all our salons in painting and sculpture....The beauty of his works and their virility will bring them always a sure triumph."

Andrew was so flattered by this praise that he sent his father the article. O'Connor released it to the Worcester Telegram, a newspaper that was always eager to print anything new about the sculptors O'Connor.

The statue of General Lawton was unveiled on the Courthouse square of Indianapolis on May 30, 1907. An article printed in the Indianapolis newspaper of April 13, 1936, said, "Unlike much other biographical sculpture of the period, which generally has about as much life as a cast iron deer on lawns, this figure has a living quality."

Among those seated on the platform at the dedication were President Theodore Roosevelt, a good friend of Lawton, and James Whitcomb Riley, who read a poem, *"The Home Voyage."*

In late 1905 Stanford White had visited O'Connor's studio. He had come to Paris to see his long-time client, James Gordon Bennett, owner of the New York Herald Tribune, who wanted to finalize plans for a family burial vault which had been under discussion since 1903. Bennett owned a large plot of land in the Washington Heights section of upper Manhattan overlooking the Hudson River, where he planned to raise a monument in the shape of an owl - the figure that had been used by his father years before on the roof of the Herald Tribune Newspaper.

This was to be a grandiose project that would rival the Statue of Liberty in size.

Appearing in the Boston Transcript of May 28,1928 was O'Connor's version of the owl story. Since he was the only one alive of the three people involved, O'Connor was happy to put down his tools and chat with the reporter. "As was well known, the Bennett coat of arms was an owl... and...James Gordon Bennett used to wear a little watch charm representing the owl which had belonged to his father, the founder of the Herald. When he first went to Stanford White with his project of an enormous owl monument, he showed Mr. White his charm.

"I want something of this sort, only on a large scale", he said. He had the monument definitely in his mind. The owl was to be on a pedestal 75 feet high and would overlook the city. of New York.

Made of bronze, its eyes were to have two great lights inside like lighthouse lamps. A coffin was to be hung from the inside top by chains. In the pedestal a circular staircase, continuing up to the top of the owl, would wind around the suspended coffin, which would have enough room around it so that no one would be able to reach it with a cane or umbrella. "Stanford White, of whom I saw a good deal at the time (1903), as I was living in New York, asked me to do the owl, and he was to make the pedestal.

"I was tremendously interested and agreed to do it, but the first thing I discovered when I went to work was that I knew nothing about owls. So for a long time I studied them. Do you know they are queer animals - owls. They look like a cat, but they have no legs like this." O'Connor took out his pencil and sketched rapidly the outline of an owl. You see, it does very well for a watch charm, but not at all when enlarged to several hundred times that size." From O'Connor's rapid sketch it was easy to see how ungainly a seventy five foot realistic owl would look.

"After studying for some time with Lucius Beebe, who was then writing a book on them, I decided too make a statue which would be suggestive of an owl and at the same time be monumental. I became much interested in the problem and made a sketch.

"Both White and I worked on the pedestal. I made one which was larger at the base and decorated with a scarab, while his was oblong in shape and contained a row of statues underneath the owl. We chose his and decided to place two white lions by the door. Then we sent for Bennett who was in Paris.

"He answered he would come right over on his yacht. He sailed across from France, entered New York harbor, and then, deciding not to land, went on down to Cuba. You know he hated New York like poison. From Cuba he sent for the sketches." He didn't like the sketches. He said, *If America should be buried and in 2000 years this statue should be dug up, it would look not like an American but and Egyptian thing.* Of course that was true." He then asked them to make another but they lost interest in 1903, and it was not until White visited Paris in 1905 that they once again began discussing the owl.

White's earliest studies were for a bronze owl 60 feet high placed on a 55 foot high pedestal; later the owl was to be 80 feet high on a similar pedestal. In 1905 when White visted Bennett in Paris, the owl had grown to 100 feet in their conversations. The idea obviously dwarfed all other plans of burial by men of wealth and it also insured Bennett that he would not be snatched after death and be held for ransom as had happened to A.T. Steward, the department store magnate.

The final owl that O'Connor designed had been approved by Bennett, and Andrew was to execute the finished plan. Its details subject to frequent correction were the subject of massive communication between the three.....Finally, "The owl must look ferocious and scowl at everyone.

When Stanford White finished his business with Bennett in Paris in 1905, he stopped by to tell O'Connor that the project was almost finalized and they would be starting soon. They were both excited and intrigued with the impending work, discussing the type of stone for the pedestal, where it could be found, transportation to the site and all manner of things pertinent to the subject. When White left to go back to America, plans were made to sign the contracts. The design and a small model remained in White's possession in readiness for the final go-ahead.

Stanford White was well known for the help he gave to struggling artists. In his profession he was able to commission whom ever he thought would do the best work for a particular undertaking. He was interested in designing in the European style as well as embracing the art of his own country.

One young artist whom White assisted was named Gertrude Vanderbilt Whitney, 31. She was married to Harry Payne Whitney, and mother of three children. On invitation White went to her studio to look at one of her sculptures, admittedly "with a little dread." He was, however, "taken off my feet." on entering the studio, by the life-like appearance of the study, -its vigor and poise. When Mrs. Whitney asked who he thought was the best teacher to give her lessons in modelling, White recommended her to Daniel Chester French as a "charming girl with a real talent for sculpture" and suggested that he would take it as a favor if she could study with French for a few weeks before she would be going abroad.

French took her on for a few weeks and she "enjoyed the lessons tremendously." It is conceivable that she knew Andrew Jr. at this time as well as other artists and sculptors who worked in and around MacDougal Alley in New York city. She was also familiar with his work, dating from the St. Bartholomew Doors that he had done for her mother.

Maurice Guillemot visited the O'Connor atelier often and had seen the design of Andrew's owl. He had generally set his seal of approval on this Worcester boy without reservation. "There is in O'Connor an energy - a sort of brutality, that will easily triumph over a certain mannerism which does not belong to him. The clean shaven face, the high brow, crowned with ruddy and rebellious locks, the vigorous torso, the powerful hands, the great energy concealed under an outward timidity, the sincere convictions and sane ambition shining in the clear glance give testimony of a man who goes straight to his aim; of a strong will and progressive instincts." He pointed out that O'Connor's chief idols were Donalette and Rodin, and it was the latter who had the most influence upon him. "He actually shares in some of the gifts of the incomparable master - that of a cunning distribution of lights and shadows."

It was not long after Hector's birth that Jesse became pregnant again, and Owen was born in 1906. He was named for Andrew's grandfather. Life was so busy for Jesse with two children under the age of two, a nursemaid was hired to help - and give her a little free time. Andrew became extremely busy as well, putting on a one man exhibit in Munich, Germany at the Kunst Salon of Walther Zimmerman. As with all else, the profession of sculpturing flourished with exposure and advertising.

In his studio a bust of *Daphne,* also called *La Fauness* was in progress. The bronze head was twelve inches high. It was modeled after Jesse, but the features were purposely made courser.

On June 25th, 1906, the world was shocked by the news that Stanford White had been shot to death on the rooftop of Madison Square Garden, a building that he had designed and enjoyed visiting for its unusual restaurant on the roof. White's personal life had apparently led to his murder. During his playboy days, he had engaged in an affair with Evelyn Nesbit, a well known and beautiful model in New York city. After the affair was over and they had drifted in other directions, Evelyn married Harry Thaw, a wealthy, but mentally unstable gentleman, who suspected that White was still involved with his wife. Often to tease him, Nesbit made veiled references about White, for she still loved him.

Thaw, who hired detectives to follow White became familiar with his habits and favorite places. One of these being the Madison Square Garden. One evening he followed him there, and as Stanny sat at a table, Thaw approached, shot point blank killing him instantly.

On hearing the sad news, Andrew was extremely affected. Death was not something that he rationalized well, and a violent one was something he could not understand at all. Since he had been with his friend so recently, he found it difficult to accept the finality of Stanford White's death. James Gordon Bennet took the news as a bad omen and immediately cancelled all plans for the owl monument. Without Stanford White's help, O'Connor could not have accomplished this tremendous task.

Stanford White was obviously colorful as an individual and was an example of his time, when money flowed freely, and the rich believed that the world was their oyster. He was however, a hard worker who became famous for his many commissions. His lifestyle and his talent for self promotion were characteristically American. His passion for beauty and aesthetices was a part of American life beginning in the 1890's and continuing to the present day. His extravagance, self indulgence and pleasure seeking, probably mirrored society in America after some of its inhabitants no longer had to perform physical labor to attain their comforts.

Late in 1906 had Andrew sculpted a beautiful maquette in plaster, somewhat similar to one he had worked on at the French studio, perhaps to keep the idea fresh in his mind. He found it convenient to have in his inventory, when in 1909 a competition was open to sculptors of Irish descent for a monument to Commodore John Barry, whom the Irish preferred to think of as the father of the American navy. This monument was to be placed in Washington, D.C. O'Connor's maquette consisted of a free standing statue of Commodore Barry on a pedestal in front of a pool. Behind the pool stretched a frieze with free standing groups at either end.

Because Commodore Barry was born in County Wexford, Ireland and had emigrated to America, the theme of the monument was the suffering of Ireland and the resultant emigration of her people. A frieze illustrated various episodes from Ireland's history, and the two free standing groups represented *Exile from Ireland.* A seated female figure of the motherland was surrounded by her sons that he named *The Genius of Ireland.* The models had been completed, and the maquette was offered to the commissioners for their approval. When the decision came as to whom they would give the commission, O'Connor's 'Barry maquette' was not selected. It was considered too shocking in its depiction of naked Irish emigrants or the Barry family preferred to think of their ancestor as a gentleman, and O'Connor had portrayed him as an ordinary seaman. In any event, he was disappointed that he wouln't be finishing and dedicating the maquette. Commodore Barry, as an individual statue was exhibited and eventually sold.

Commodore John Barry Maquette.

Every year Andrew had to plan his entry for the spring opening of the Salon. In 1907 his exhibit was a plaster copy of his *Recuillement,* the bronze that sits in Sleepy Hollow Cemetery.

In his studio, he was working on a bas relief that he called *Jeuness*, while at home, another baby boy arrived and was named Roderick. If life was exciting with a toddler and one baby, with an additional baby it was even more exhausting for Jesse.

In 1907 Andrew worked on two statues of men that he named *The Toilers.* Six feet tall, one was a miner, the other a farmer. He had employed a studio assistant, Aristide Maen a sixteen year old local boy, and when there wasn't enough work to keep him busy, Andrew had him pose for the male statues. Although these were not commissioned by anyone, they were put aside after they were put into plaster, to be used at a later time.

Another good friend was torn from the fabric of Andrew's life when Augustus St. Gaudens died on August 3, 1907. He had been ill with cancer for many years, after having been operated

44.

on for a tumor early in the decade. When he heard about his friend and one of America's foremost sculptors, Andrew surely remembered the words of praise St. Gaudens had spoken of him; "Ah, this man is in a class by himself. I am glad the mantle is to fall on one so worthy."

The untimely death of St. Gaudens best friend Stanny, and the resultant chaos and scandal that followed may well have affected St. Gauden's spirits and hastened his death as well. The papers had been full of blame and speculation month after month, chastising White for his own death.

Worcester County people were fond of O'Connor Sr., and always eager to hear news about him and his famous son. On April 15, 1908, the Worcester Telegram carried the announcement of a farewell dinner for Andrew O'Connor Sr. prior to his surprise move to Paris. Quoting the Telegram: "The father of Andrew O'Connor of Paris, who is perhaps the most celebrated young American sculptor in the world today, will be entertained by Worcester friends at a farewell dinner tonight before he leaves for Paris, where, with his family, he will make his home with his distinguished son..hereafter."

O'Connor Sr. had finished a Civil War memorial for the town of Spencer, Massachusetts. It was a six to seven foot woman on a tall pedestal with bronze bas reliefs on either side of the pedestal depicting Civil War battle scenes. It is an impressive statue that stands on a hill in the center of the town. His cemetery monument business had been flourishing, so he felt that he could afford this trip to Paris. His son had been urging him to come for some time, and he missed Andrew Jr. There were also three small grandchildren to become acquainted with, as well. He didn't know what work he would have in Europe, but was confident that he could find something to keep him busy. O'Connor Sr. and Cora would sail for France from New York by the Red Star Line with their now fourteen year old daughter, Mildred.

O'Connor Sr. told reporters that his son had leased two houses in the Clamart district of Paris. He, Cora and Mildred would live in one of them. The arrangement seemed most convenient

Civil War Monument.
Spencer, Massachusetts.

General Lew Wallace.
Lew Wallace Library,
Crawfordsville, Indiana.

for Andrew Jr. as well. Jesse's life was not easy, being pregnant again, and with three small children, they could use the extra help that Mildred and Cora might offer. They had recently moved from the Boulevard Garibaldi to 17 Rue de Bievre, Clamart, where they were leasing a large house with a small guest house in the rear. They had enough space now, to easily accomodate two families.

There must have been great excitement when the two men were reunited after three years apart. Andrew Jr. and Jesse as well as their three children were now speaking French, a hurdle that his father, Cora and Mildred faced.

Determined to exhibit at the Salon every year, Andrew Jr. placed his bronze bust of Robert Loftin Newman, executed in 1898, and his Italian girl, *Une Calebraise* in the Salon of 1909. He had not received any commissions in Europe up to that time. D.C.French and Cass Gilbert, the architect, were both active in getting him work in the U.S., and it was through Gilbert that he was given the commission for the General Lew Wallace memorial. A full size statue of the General in marble was to be presented to the U.S.Congress by the State of Indiana to be placed in the Hall of Statues in the United States Capitol.

General Wallace was an amazing man. He was born in Brookville, Indiana, in 1827. At the age of nineteen he organized one of the first troops from the State to fight in the Mexican War. He became a lawyer by studying with his father, and served as a prosecuting attorney prior to his marriage to Susan Elston.

In 1856 he served one term in the Indiana State Senate. At the outbreak of the Civil War, he was appointed Adjutant General of Indiana, and resigned soon after, accepting a commission as Colonel of the Eleventh Indiana Volunteer Infantry. He advanced to the rank of Major General within a year and is said to have prevented the Confederate capture of Cincinnati without a battle. By delaying General Early at Monocacy, he also helped prevent an attack on Washington, D.C. by Confederate forces.

In 1865 he was second in command of the court martial that tried the President Lincoln assassination conspirators. A year later he

46.

was president of the court that tried Henry Wirz, commander of Andersonville prison. From 1878 to 1881 Lew Wallace served as the Governor of New Mexico Territory, and was the United States Minister to Turkey from 1881 to 1885.

General Wallace wrote *The Fair God* in 1870 the immortal *Ben Hur* in 1880, and the *Prince of India* in 1893. He was a talented artist and his paintings were exhibited around the country. He enjoyed music and not only played, but built violins.

After the marble statue of Lew Wallace was finished for Washington, the town of Crawfordsville, Indiana decided to purchase the study Wallace had designed and built, along with the three and a half acres of land surrounding it, and put up a bronze copy of the monument. The life-size statue stands today where the beech tree stood under which General Wallace sat as he wrote *Ben Hur* and which subsequently became known as the Ben Hur beech. The Wallace museum houses the mementos of the General's life and is listed in the National Register of Historic Places as a national landmark.

Andrew Jr. was not only eager to show the sights of Paris to his father, Cora and Mildred, but he wanted his father to see the studio of Auguste Rodin to view the works that had been so inspiring to him. When Rodin had come to know this young man and his work, he became fond of him and often visited the O'Connors at home. Although O'Connor never took any formal lessons from Rodin, it is certainly conceivable that his advice was asked and given. A visit to one of Rodin's ateliers was exciting - not only because of what could be seen, but also, what might be heard. Rodin had a way with words. He talked about art and life in a way that people remembered. Every artist who came to Paris after 1900 had to come to terms with Rodin. He was the patriarch presiding over the sculpture section of the Societe Nationale. Whether or not he chose to notice a new sculptor's work could mean success - or not for the artist. Rodin was at odds with a great deal of modern art and life. As he grew older he passed more and more hours discussing art with writers, and fewer actively producing it. Andrew was eager to hear all Rodin's theories and firmly believed it was this method he wanted to emulate.

In 1909, Jesse and Andrew's last son was born and was named Patrick, a delightful child who became known for all of his life as Paddy. The baby was enjoyed by the whole family. The children were growing fast and Andrew realized that soon there would no longer be babies. He therefore sculpted in marble, the two youngest, Patrick and Roderick, with their mother, naming the finished piece *Maternity*. Done in the style of Rodin, the three subjects seem to be emerging from the rough stone as fragile and delicate sprites. The contrast between the rough natural surface of the rock and the carefully shaped and polished faces of the figures creates an illusion that the great mass of stone behind the children is doing as much to protect and shield them as their mother is. There is little evidence of Daniel Chester French's influence here and not much of Rodin's either. French never left a figure unfinished and Rodin only left his grotesques semi-complete.

A beautiful bust of the Virgin in bronze was conceived at this time, using one of the earlier face casts of Jesse that Andrew had put aside in his studio. A plaster copy of the General Lew Wallace statue was entered in the 1909 Paris Salon, for O'Connor wanted the public, the judges and those who came to purchase works, to be aware that he was still producing fine work, even though he had not received a commission from anyone in France since he arrived. Perhaps, the reasoning was, that there were so many statues in Europe already; also the Ecole des Beaux Arts graduated many sculptors every year.

In 1909 three more statues were completed. A statue of *Adam and Eve* in marble, a marble bas-relief called *Ascension* and the statue of a female that he called *Feu Sacre* or *Sacred Fire*.

With his father's help, he put on a one man exhibit at the Galerie A. Hebrand in Paris. O'Connor was accomplishing a phenomenal amount of work.

In 1910 the O'Connors moved once again, this time to 10 Rue du Montoir, Clamart. This year the *Adam and Eve* was exhibited at the Salon, and Andrew Jr. was asked to represent Great Britain at the Venice Biennale.

Maternity. Jesse holding Roderick and Patrick.

Adam and Eve in marble.
by Andrew O'Connor Jr.

By permission of the
Corcoran Gallery of Art.
Washington, D.C.

Gift of Edward Tuck.

Early in 1911 Andrew was asked to submit a small maquette for an equestrian monument to General Alvear, destined for Buenos Aires. Although the maquette he prepared was well done, the commissioners rejected it, and O'Connor ruefully considered the time and effort spent on it, a waste. On the heels of the General Alvear memorial came the request for an idea of a monument to honor Governor John Albert Johnson of St. Paul, Minnesota.

O'Connor had been recommended by his friend, Cass Gilbert, who was born in Zanesville, Ohio, and moved to St. Paul at an early age. In preparing for the Johnson memorial, O'Connor read about the popular Governor. John Albert Johnson died in Rochester, Minnesota on September 21, 1909, as the result of an operation. The serious nature of his illness was realized only a few days before the end, and the suspense with which bulletins were awaited, created an intensity of feeling and sympathy that came to a climax when his death was announced on the morning of September 21. The people's grief was overwhelming. A suggestion that a memorial statue should be placed before the capitol in St. Paul was printed in a local newspaper, the Pioneer Press, which immediately set up a fund with a limit of a dollar from each person in St. Paul who wanted to contribute to the monument. Other leading newspapers throughout the state also began to receive contributions. At a meeting of the Executive Committee the Secretary submitted a list of forty sculptors who had been suggested to do the statue. The committee chose five people from the list by a process of elimination. The Secretary then wrote to Mr. O'Connor and the four others asking them to submit sketches.

In the summer of 1910, Cass Gilbert and a Mr. Ames visited O'Connor's Paris studio to inspect his sketches. The designs were then sent to the committee for their inspection. On October 25, 1910, at the St. Paul Institute, the committee decided that O'Connor's design of the monument not be accepted after they examined the sketches and model carefully. They had not decided on the monument by the end of the year, so on January 23, 1911, O'Connor appeared in St. Paul, with new designs for a detached monument to be considered by the Executive Committee, who then accompanied O'Connor to the State Capitol to view the grounds for possible sites for the memorial..

The Commission met five days later and approved the recommendations of the Executive Committee to sign a contract with him for the memorial. It was agreed that the sum to be paid would be $21,500. The collection was a fund of nearly $25,000. A larger fund could have been raised by removing the limitation of the amount. There were many people in the state who would have been glad to give larger sums for the monument. It was felt that Governor Johnson was best honored by individuals with equal donations.

The completed statues arrived in St. Paul in September of 1912, and O'Connor followed in October to supervise setting up the monument on its pedestal. The standing Governor John Albert Johnson is flanked at his feet by two men on each side called *The Toilers.* On his left stand the *Miner* and the *Blacksmith* on the right, the *Timber Cruiser* and the *Farmer.* The statue itself is nine feet tall on a ten foot high pedestal. The two groups are each six feet tall. Since two of the *Toilers* were created earlier and were in his inventory, it was comparatively easy to do two more in the same configuration below the standing figure of Governor Johnson. The statue posed for by Aristide Maen would finally be set up in a public place.

52.   Governor John Albert Johnson and The Toilers.
State House, St. Paul, Minnesota.

V

Gertrude Vanderbilt Whitney

Gertrude Vanderbilt Whitney was a five-foot-eight inch svelte young woman with green eyes, brown hair and a fair complexion. When O'Connor met her, she was married to millionaire Harry Payne Whitney and had three children. Although she was described by some as "plain," her dark hair and fresh, rosy complexion made her look striking.

Gertrude was the daughter of millionaire Cornelius Vanderbilt, and the greatest problem of her young life seemed to be too much money. While she was being courted by Harry Payne Whitney, she wrote in her diary: "You don't know what the position of an heiress is! You can't imagine. There is no-one in all the world who loves her for herself. She cannot do this, that, and the other simply because she is known by sight and will be talked about...everyone she loves, loves her for what she has got, and earth is hell unless she is a fool, and then it's heaven.." With this philosophy she went on in her life to 'use' people as well as the reverse.

Harry and Gertrude Whitney were married at the Breakers, the family summer cottage in Newport, Rhode Island. Although very much in love in the beginning, he gradually found his own interests. As children came along, she in self-preservation, turned to sculpting and other men. She had outfitted a studio on MacDougal Alley in 1907 two years after O'Connor left for Europe. By 1912 She had a studio in Paris as well as one on another of her properties in Westbury, Long Island. NY.

In 1912 Gertrude wrote a note to O'Connor asking if she could visit his studio and view his work. He answered her note, giving her a morning appointment. When she arrived, he showed her the work he had in progress and also some peices that had been finished and not sold. As she wrote in her diary, she thought that his work was "big and strong, and full of meaning like himself."

She then invited him to her studio for advice about her sculpture. If Andrew could have known that his well ordered world was about to be turned upside down, he would have fled in fright. Although Gertrude had been acquainted with Andrew O'Connor for seven or eight years, since the time he had done the St. Bartholomew doors for her mother, she did not know him well.

She recorded in her diary entry of February 29th. "When something comes to one out of a clear sky, a beautiful thing that one has no right to expect, a thing of meaning which one has done nothing to deserve - when this happens - no matter what the result may be, one sings a song of praise. It has happened to me. And the reason that I put this great value on what I have been given is because I want and need it. It's the breath of my life. It's happiness. It's the lost complement of myself that I have found."

Andrew went to her studio a few times, gave advice and they talked. He stayed longer than he should have. He hardly ever sat down, being in the habit of standing at his work, and probably very nervous, he walked about as he talked. Even though she knew her work wasn't great, he was encouraging about it. Twice he had lunch with her in the first days of their friendship, but he never seemed to be more than just interested in her. She began paying him for lessons, so he would come over when he had time. In her diary she wrote; "Of course I knew he was interested in me, found me sympathetic, but that's all I thought. I liked him right away, his apparent sincerity, his tastes and loves which he scarcely needed to express, I knew so well. The beginning of one of our sentences always suggested the end to the other."

One day O'Connor came to her studio about eleven o'clock. As she worked on a nude male figure using a model, he pointed out things she should be doing differently. He stayed for lunch and they chatted. He told her that he enjoyed coming and giving her lessons because she was so enthusiastic. He was beginning to warm up to her, but resisted her advances. She herself had been posing nude for a sculptor friend, and after her own model had left late in the afternoon, she showed Andrew the photographs of the statue her friend was sculpting. As she wrote in her diary, "He was struck, serious, intent. He said they were among the most beautiful things he had ever seen. I felt then, his great and real admiration at least for my physique."

Gertrude Vanderbilt Whitney.

They stood together conversing late into the afternoon and enjoyed watching the sun set. Then she sat on the sofa, hoping he would sit beside her, but he continued to stand close by as they talked. She wanted to pull him down next to her. suddenly he stared at her with a strange look, fighting the instincts that told him he must leave. He leaned against the sofa, and she made room for him to sit. It was dark, but she made no move to put on the light. They could barely see the outlines of each other, and Andrew felt himself being drawn into a situation he couldn't resist, much as a fly must feel when he realizes he's caught in a spider's web.

To her diary Gertrude later confided: "A fearfully strong feeling came over me to lean against him while he talked... It will come, we will care, it must be."

After some time, they got up and Andrew was surprised to see that it was seven o'clock and mentioned that he thought he would take a walk on the boulevards. "Take me," she said, and he began talking some more, playing for time to decide whether to pursue this dangerous path. Finally, he seemed to make up his mind as he asked, "Aren't you coming?"

Gertrude hurried to change into a black velvet dress that she thought he might like, and threw on a pair of shoes that she didn't have time to lace properly. When she returned to the other room, he noticed them, bent down and laced them for her. They set off for the streets of Paris like two children who were just let out of school.

He took her to a secluded spot, Moorish-style, down a small alley just off the Boulevard, and they had dinner, while he told her that he thought her very intelligent, which of course she was, but perhaps because she had the time to listen intently while he spoke and hung on every word. There were no youngsters running about as there were when he talked with Jesse. He thought her beautiful, without rationalizing that she had the resources to be so. He told her that of all the things in the world, he preferred being with her.

The relationship progressed to a more intimate level, as a later notation in her diary attested. She began calling him her Dream Man, perhaps so that if anyone read her diary they wouldn't suspect the relationship. She wrote that he had told her she was at her prime, and that now was the time that she must pursue her career seriously and ride the crest of the wave. He said he believed in her ability to produce with his help, the best anyone could do in sculpture.

1912 was an idyllic time for Gertrude and Andrew. He was at her studio frequently, correcting her work and teaching her how to improve. When she became frustrated with her work, she would exclaim that he should do it all, and then it would be done well. O'Connor was being paid well for teaching Gertrude, but much more than that was involved. In a letter to Andrew she wrote, "I want so much and you ... have even for the eighth of a second given it all to me...You are the only thing that counts and I love you as one does when all the padding is out. I hate this life of pretense...Dear Love, I want to run to you, to leave the absurdity of the world. If I had no children I would give up all things...you told me one afternoon in the studio how I must never forget that you loved me for good and all...Good night, Dream Man, I love you always..."

For a while when they lived in Clamart, the painter Robert Loftin Newman lived with them. Not only was he there long enough to do his own painting, but also for Andrew to finish a bronze portrait bust of him. He was an exceedingly handsome man with a beard, mustache and fine head of hair.

O'Connor Sr. and Cora were not happy in Paris. Homesick for the rest of the family, they took Mildred and returned to the United States and Holden, Massachusetts.

Jesse was having a difficult time with Andrew gone so frequently. The boys were more of a handful as they grew. There were times that he didn't come home in time for dinner after being away all day. This made an already suspicious and jealous Jesse even more concerned. She couldn't complain too loudly however, since there was now a steady income and she didn't have the continuous worry about how she would pay the largest of bills, but she wasn't happy with her life. She sensed a change in their lives with each other. She knew her chances were slim of keeping Andrew in her world after he had been exposed to the luxury, and atmosphere where one need not worry about the next dollar.

There were two sculptures in progress at Gertrude's studio in 1912. One, the nude of a standing male athlete with one hand gripping the back of his head in a contorted gesture of *Despair,* the title of the piece, The other was the most ambitious piece she had yet attempted, a fountain commissioned for the new Arlington Hotel in Washington, D.C. This involved three male figures, slightly larger than life, supporting a basin of leaves, grapes and fish, about eleven feet in diameter. This commission needed much of O'Connor's expertise, and he was not satisfied with it until it was finished properly.

At the 1912 Salon, O'Connor exhibited a fragment of the Governor Johnson Monument, one of the two-man groups. Also the marble bust of Edward Tuck. The Salon was an inspiration to an artist to keep producing new works whether he won a prize or not, and no matter how busy he was with other projects, Andrew made certain that he would have a piece of sculpture for exhibition every Spring.

In October, O'Connor was in St. Paul, Minnesota arranging the Governor Johnson statue on its pedestal, and the unveiling ceremony. Back at home, he finished a work called *Monument Funeraire en Pierre*. (Funeral Monument in stone). This was copied from the *Recuillement* design, sculpted in granite.

During the Spring of 1913 O'Connor was hospitalized for an operation. Complications kept him off his feet for several weeks while he recuperated. News traveled fast, and D.C. French who heard of his misfortune, wrote to him, offering to "guide a commission into your skillful hands."

The proposed work was for four tablets for an art building. French wrote: "I told him [the commissioner] that I could not do them for a good while, in any case, and that it was a kind of thing that I had not had much experience in. I recommended that he should apply to you. He told me that he had thought of you but did not know where to reach you; so after all you are not particularly indebted to me." French mentioned another man who had come to his studio a day or two after this, and he had given him O'Connor's name as well. He hoped that one of the two jobs would materialize. He suggested that there was not much work to be found in Paris, while America was still looking for monuments for its parks and squares. Suggesting O'Connor was better off at home.

In early 1914, O'Connor received another letter from French, who was offering him the commission for another statue and wanted O'Connor to give him a price. He suggested that it would be all right to put a good price on it, as the money was available to pay for it. He mentioned that his opinion had been sought as to who was a good sculptor and he had recommended O'Connor. He didn't know if they would take his suggestion, but, "I shall take pleasure in sounding your praises to the best of my ability."

Following this letter, O'Connor sent photographs of his latest work along with a letter indicating that he would like the work, but could not meet the deadline that the Committee had set. French, of course, did not know that O'Connor was not only doing his own work but also was in the employ of Mrs.

Whitney and was therefore burdened by the deadlines imposed by other Commissioners.

Not knowing the complete story, French wrote a typically fatherly letter on April 15, scolding O'Connor. He then went on to say that he had received the pictures of his latest work. "I appreciate your feeling in not wishing to have the Committee judge your work or put any limitation of time upon you, and I am confident that it would be for the good of sculpture if this rule could obtain, but naturally and from their point of view at least very properly, the Committee must have something to say about the work which they pay for.

"There is a difference between giving the statue all the thought and time that are required ... there are plenty of cases where the best results have not been served by the lapse of time required for the production of the statue."

French was on this committee and offered to be an arbiter. Would it be possible for O'Connor to name a reasonable time for completion of the piece and would he please agree to have the statue commission subject to approval of said committee.?

He noted that O'Connor could not expect to get the commission if these conditions were not met. He had intended to speak earnestly on O'Connor's behalf in order to get him the work, but he didn't care to do so unless O'Connor would accept the conditions that the commission stipulated, because he felt it would be hopeless. He continued the letter with the thought;

"I am sure that if you were over here you would have all the work that you could possibly do, and it is an awful pity that a man of your great talent should not be permitted to give to the world all the art that is in him. It seems an awful waste of good material." French remarked that he had been to the Knoedler exhibit in New York where he had seen Mrs. Whitney's fountain of three male figures. He thought the figures "certainly very handsome" and had heard rumors that O'Connor had helped her with it "which accounts for a good deal." In a postscript he mentioned that twelve to fifteen thousand dollars would be paid for the statue that was to be commissioned. He closed as usual, with the words

"Yours Faithfully".

O'Connor answered this letter, but did not mention the Whitney fountain or explain his part in it.

The desire for monuments in America seemed to be on the rise. On May 14, 1914, French wrote another letter to O'Connor telling him about two statues that would be coming along for bid. The Committee in this case was looking for photographs of O'Connor's work.

French had given them the names of six sculptors who were capable, advising all of them to submit photos. He urged O'Connor to mention in his return letter that he would be sending the pictures, and then he, French, would furnish pictures immediately, as he had a collection of O'Connor's work. Of course, French emphasized, everything depended upon whether he wanted the work or not.

He said that he had received O'Connor's letter of the 26th of April, and was "glad to know that a bribe of twelve or fifteen thousand dollars will seduce you into giving up your high and mighty principles." He thought it not too much to ask a sculptor to give a completion estimate of his work. D.C. French was beginning to understand what Andrew was doing and it disturbed him, for by now, Andrew was doing more on Gertrude's work than just advising and teaching. He was actually sculpting much of her statues.

Apparently, O'Connor told French about his deep affection for Rodin and his work. This prompted French to remark: "Your temperamental affections about Rodin are noted. I have been wondering whether you remember that I was largely instrumental in getting the collection of his works for the (Metropolitan) museum." In 1910, French had taken his wife and daughter to Paris on a vacation, but also to pick out some of Rodin's best works for an exhibit in the Metropolitan Museum in New York. He had visited O'Connor's studio at the time.

O'Connor was now finishing a portrait bust of Madame X. Over the years the Madame in question was thought to be either a Russian Countess or the wife of a midwest banker.

60.

She was identified by Patrick, as a woman of the night and literally, a Madame known as Suzy. While he was sculpting *Madame X,* Roderick was painting her portrait. O'Connor was also working on *The Virgin in Stone,* in the style of Rodin. He had finished a pensive, sad portrait bust called *The Exile.* Both of these were done from the masks of Jesse that he had made nine years before, but perhaps noting her current pensive facial expressions reflecting her sadness. It seems strange that deep into his affair with Gertrude, Andrew was reaching back to his beginnings with Jesse to do works that were not commissioned.

If O'Connor didn't go to her studio, Gertrude felt completely comfortable coming to O'Connor's and was a guest that the children grew accustomed to seeing. She was frequently at the house and the children, at any rate, liked her.

In her last year in Paris before war came, Gertrude wrote a letter to a friend in New York. She said that she had been working very hard on three sketches and had taken only one afternoon off to go with O'Connor to his studio at Clamart where she viewed his beautiful work: "for there is nobody whose things I admire more." He was planning a group for her studio at Westbury, Long Island and she was interested in seeing the sketch of it, very impressed with his ideas.

While in Paris Gertrude frequently saw the sculptors Haseltine, Rosales and O'Connor, all reputedly on her payroll. She was most involved with O'Connor and wrote twenty one pages in her diary about their relationship, concluding: "I found something in you which I had never possessed and I longed to have it. So after awhile I held out my arms and it came. You gave me part of yourself. You talked to me. You told me about what you were going to do. You talked in another dimension."

Although O'Connor did most of the finish work on the statues, Gertrude's designs were her own, as were the small clay models. Another large nude male figure she was doing was named *Titanic.* In a letter to O'Connor in 1914, she mentioned that in a few days the foundry would have her memorial bronzed and she would be seeing it twelve feet high. She hoped that he would like it, and that's all she cared about.

Back in New York the art community around MacDougal Alley was buzzing with the controversy surrounding O'Connor's work on Mrs. Whitney's sculptures, and she assuming the credit. It was a shady area, for didn't the greatest sculptors send their small plaster models to Italy to have them carved into life size marble statues? The argument here, probably was that O'Connor was correcting and finishing the original clay models, putting them into plaster and guiding the job right through to the foundry. Mrs. Whitney was then taking the bows for the finished product. The original promise that Andrew made of making her a famous sculptor was not meant to be done in a way that would compromise himself.

Americans living in Europe in the spring of 1914 never really believed that there was going to be a war. Gradually as they became aware, their ranks thinned. Nevertheless, the O'Connors were still there when Aristide Maen, their studio aide, left to join the French army.

One day a brigade of soldiers marched down the road and stopped before the house to salute the family as they stood at the window waving. The news soon came that France had declared war on Germany, and on August 3, 1914, the German army was not far from Paris. The family could hear the dull thunder of cannon, as they hurriedly packed everything and left for the United States and Washington, D.C. where O'Connor had been commissioned a statue to honor Robert Emmet, an Irish patriot who had died in 1803.

Gertrude stayed in Paris and made arrangements to purchase O'Connor's studio at 51 Rue Boileau.

After a year in Washington, Andrew's work was finished and at his father's urging, he took his family to Paxton, a small town in Massachusetts located next to the town of Holden. Sr. had arranged for his son to buy the Hadley house and was overjoyed that finally the family would be closer.

VI

Paxton, Massachusetts

The house in Paxton was a large two story farmhouse with a massive fireplace in the living room and four bedrooms upstairs. Andrew immediately proposed modernizing two bathrooms in the house with tile floor and new fixtures. The front windows looked out over the city of Worcester in the distance and in the same direction, closer still, the sunken garden and apple orchard. Set at the top end of forty five acres, it was quiet and peaceful.

Andrew Jr. immediately set to work using the stable as a temporary studio. A fireplace kept it warm in the cold weather while a local carpenter worked to his specifications building a studio next to the house. He knew what he wanted, and designing it gave him ample opportunity to incorporate his own ideas and some that he had admired in French's studio.

The commission on which he had bid, for a Spanish War Memorial for the city of Worcester was awarded to O'Connor Jr. and work was immediately begun. He named the statue '1898' or *The Spanish War Memorial*. O'Connor Sr. was also busy. He had been awarded the commission for a fountain for the city. A design he had submitted to the Park Department had been accepted. When the statue was finished and dedicated the Worcester Magazine of September 1915 wrote: "The story of Worcester's second and latest memorial fountain dates back to 1910 when Mrs. Louisa B. Chamberlain, widow of Dr. William B. Chamberlain, a widely known homeopathic physician, consulted with Frederick A. McClure, city engineer in regard to a bequest that she had in mind. The Chamberlain home was for many years on Elm Street, Worcester, opposite the public library, and both Dr. Chamberlain and his wife were much attached to the horses that headed their own stable equipment and to the various animal pets of the household."

"The fountain had to be erected within two years after the receipt of the money from her estate. The amount for the statue would be five thousand dollars and the approval of the design rested entirely with Mr. McClure.

Of all the drawings for the fountain and the models of the figure to be placed on top that were submitted by sculptors in the city, the design of O'Connor Sr. was approved immediately and he received the commission. As the magazine article continues, "It is a pleasing conception of the sculptor which transmits in flowing lines of bronze the figure of a sturdy boy who stands upon the brink of a mimic brook that spouts beneath his feet." Dressed in a bathing suit, he seems to have climbed up on the side of the stream and is preparing to bait his hook and throw his fishing line into the pool. The figure is lifelike, posed by Francis Kittredge, the youngest son of the man who designed the beautiful granite base.

The drinking fountain is carved from pink Milford granite. It is oblong and contains six bowls through which water passes. In the trough below the boy's figure, there is also a place where a stream pours out as if from a natural source. On each side of the base of the fountain is a drinking place for dogs who can easily reach the water from ground level.

The fountain was unveiled on August 14, 1915 with Andrew O'Connor Sr. in attendance. Although it stood for many years in front of Union Station, it was eventually moved to facilitate traffic flow, and now stands appropriately, next to the pond in Worcester's Elm Park. Sadly, early in its life, the fishing pole disappeared, leaving *The Fisher Boy* in a pugilistic stance.

The studio that Andrew Jr. was having built was on top of a hill and people traveling the highway below watched as it took shape. When the building was finished and the work moved inside, people passing along the road, looked up the hill and claimed they could see the sculptor working at the open window.

When the O'Connors arrived in Paxton, the boys were no longer babies. Patrick was five, Roderick seven, Owen eight and Hector, nine years of age. As soon as school began, the truant officer appeared at their door to find out why they were not registered at the Center School. Andrew explained that his sons were being taught at home. Thereupon, they were given lessons by their Grandpere, Andrew Sr. Their father, who was, in the words of Worcester Telegram's Margaret Getchell Parsons, "One of the most brilliant and fascinating conversationalists we have ever known in Worcester County, had many theories. One of them was that schooling as we know it today can crush the individuality of a child whout teaching him what is necessary in life.

O'Connor Sr. tutored the boys, although the word 'tutor' was a bit formal for the type of instruction he gave them. It would be more accurate to say that he directed their reading and helped to develop each of the four boys along the lines in which each showed an interest. Hector decided he would be a linguist. Owen, Patrick and Roderick were encouraged to follow whatever appealed to them. They began painting and drawing. Eventually, Andrew picked up the sketches they made and left lying about and proudly showed them to his friends. Jesse saw to it that they spent several hours a day learning the fundamentals of reading, writing and arithmetic. Andrew purchased books on the great masters, Rembrandt, Renoir and Monet and they became familiar with all of them. They had favorite painters and Rod liked Rembrandt. Patrick remembered years later that since thiis man was Rod's favorite, no one else was allowed to study his work.

Mrs. Carlson, a nearby neighbor stopped in frequently and gave Jesse advice about cooking. Sometimes her daughter Flossie tended the boys when the parents were away. To quote a rather

The Fisher Boy.
Next to the pond,
Elm Park,
Worcester, MA.

66.

lyrical story in the Worcester Telegram, one would suppose the children were angels. Margaret Parsons wrote: "Their's was a simple but charming home. When one came to call on the O'Connors, the boys would perhaps hear your car, come quietly out of the surrounding woods or fields where they had been playing, and stand nearby looking at you with their great round eyes. They were shy but they were also polite and somehow, perhaps it was their European training or the unspoiled freedom from conventional life they were then living, they did not seem like the ordinary more or less rough and tumble American youngster of the same age."

A friend remarked one day, They are like fauns, or half tamed things of the woods, the way they pop out, and in their shy but interested way, watch what is going on among these outsiders who have come to their home." If she had interviewed the baby sitter at the time, she would have heard a different story. Flossie Carlson stayed at the house with the children on a week-end when their parents went to New York. Hearing a commotion upstairs, she ran up and found a full fledged pillow fight in progress, with bits of down and feathers falling like snow everywhere. Flossie was aghast and not knowing what to do, threatened to call their parents. By the time she had located the number and gone to the phone to dial, there was no dial tone - the line had been severed.

Mrs. Carlson enjoyed telling her family about the first car that Andrew bought. Jesse could hardly wait to try it out. The first chance she got, she climbed in and shifted into reverse. Not having mastered the delicate balance between the clutch, brake, and accelerator, she gave it the gas and shot backwards over the garden wall. The car teetered precariously as she gingerly climbed out, wondering what Andrew would say when he saw it. Patrick, in his later years, fondly reminisced that "Jesse was an awful driver, even after she learned how it all worked."

One of Andrew Jr's closest friends was Maurice Reidy. They met at an O'Connor family party in Providence, Rhode Island. Reidy and O'Connor grew up in the same neighborhood and they developed a friendship warmer than that which he had with his siblings. Often on a Sunday the families of the two men had dinner together at the large dining table in Paxton. Reidy documented much of Andrew's work and took an avid interest in his new commissions. He was there for him at times when money was short, and when the loan was repaid, he would receive a bronze bust or a painting by one of the boys.

Another of his friends, the Reverend Michael Earls S.J. of Holy Cross College came into his life about this time. He had visited the studio with several others to admire Andrew's latest work, probably the Spanish War Hero. There were always statues in progress, and as the other visitors looked, asked questions about how the work was done and left, Andrew was struck by this man who merely stood quietly and gazed at it. His obvious pleasure over the sculptures impressed Andrew and they conversed. An immediate friendship developed. Father Earls at first was invited, and then began to drop by the house frequently. The family became very fond of him. Andrew began a crucifix for him out of marble and this proved to be a respite from the larger works in progress.

The statue that occupied most of Andrew's time in 1916-1917 was the *1898 or Spanish War Memorial.* An article in the Worcester Telegram of March 1944, twenty seven years after it had been dedicated notes; "Perhaps the most artistic memorial in the City of Worcester is the statue which stands in Armory Square and commemorates the soldiers of the United States who fought in the Spanish War. The Monument is called simply '1898.' It is a life-size bronze figure of a sturdy fighter in a thin loose shirt with short sleeves, no cap on his tousled hair, old pants tucked into high rough boots and a cartridge belt about his waist. One big toil-worn hand rests on his hip in a tired, relaxed pose. A gun is slung over the left shoulder."

Ms. Abercrombie of the Worcester Telegram viewed the "1898" in progress. She wrote, on visiting the studio: "O'Connor would not hesitate to put aside his tools, step back from his model, and greet visitors. He was genial and an engaging talker, with a ready wit and a gracious smile." She described him as broad shouldered and rugged in appearance.

He wore his hair long and it was usually tousled, giving the impression that he was too engrossed in work to worry about appearances. He was, however, always well-dressed and quick to speak in praise of Worcester and what his early training here had meant to him. During conversations he often referred to his father as his greatest source of inspiration.

Commenting on the latest statue, she described the 1898's casualness seen in the relaxed hand on the hip or in the wrinkling of the shirt, pants and boots. The *1898* soldier indeed portrays a new image of the American as tall, lanky and good natured.

When he began working on the memorial, O'Connor took on several art students to work with him. One was Vincent S. Wickham a student at the Normal Art School - now Massachusetts School of Art. Because Wickham was the slimmest of the students, O'Connor used him for the *1898* soldier. On April 17, 1917, the *1898* was unveiled amidst much pomp and circumstance in Worcester's Wheaton Square

One day Aristide Maen arrived from Paris He had served in the World War been wounded in the leg. When he returned, he met and wooed his sweetheart, Helene. They decided to come to the United States and stay with the O'Connors. Andrew was able to obtain the keys for the empty Boynton family farmhouse across from his own, and they moved into it. Aristide was a painter and proved to be very popular with the children in the neighborhood. They often sat for him as he painted their portraits.. He helped Andrew when needed, and, Helene was good company for Jesse. In her spare moments, Helene took it upon herself to document and photograph the sculpture that was underway in the studio with the intention of writing a book about it at some future date.

Sometime in 1918, members of the University Club of Chicago voted to erect a monument to those members who had been killed in the World War. O'Connor submitted a model and went to Chicago to view the site on which it would be placed.

70.

When the committee saw his memorial, they decided that major revisions should be made before they would accept it. O'Connor, who had enough work to keep him busy for a long while, refused to change the basic design. With deep regret, the monument was not accepted, and thus began the history of the three piece monument *Debarquement.*

The theme of the monument was the return of a hero to his native land, mourned by his wife and mother. The main figure was a soldier on a stretcher placed on a bier, next to the bier was his mother, sixty two and a half inches tall, who was to be placed at ground level, leaning her right arm near the victim's head. On the right side of the main statue, the wife, called the *Mourning Woman* is a fascinating and haunting figure. The woman kneels as if she has been in the same position for a hundred years. As Maurice Reidy said, "The head and arms seem to grow from the veiled body like branches from a gnarled tree trunk. O'Connor has made that which is not grotesque appear to be grotesque. This is the influence of Rodin. The manner in which the light plays in the many crags and uneven surfaces makes the figures appear to be made of something more than cold, black, bronze.

After ten or twelve years of traveling around from studio to studio with Andrew, the bronze trio came to rest in the Tate Museum in London. The base is inscribed: "As cranes chanting their dolorous notes traverse the sky."

There is a second *Debarquement* located in Merrion Square in Dublin where it stands next to a path winding through the Park. Martin Wood said in his book Sargent, that only a colorist loves black and sees it as a color. As O'Connor was a pupil of John Singer Sargent, it is indeed possible that he embraced the same philosophy, as indicated by the three figures of the *Debarquement.*

Soon after his return from Paris in 1915, O'Connor was invited by the Illinois Art Commission to submit a design for a statue of Abraham Lincoln. Fifty two artists sent in their ideas, forty nine were in general competition and three by invitation. The monument was to be set up in front of the new statehouse being built in Springfield, the Capitol of Illinois.

The three designs submitted by invitation were from Albert Jaegers and Herman MacNeil of New York and Andrew O'Connor of Paxton. Each received an award of five hundred dollars. There were also prizes for the best three models in the general competition. The Commissioner, keeping strictly within the bounds prescribed for the work, selected four competitors, one of whom was O'Connor, to receive an additional five hundred dollars each for enlarged models of their designs. After several months the final decision was made. O'Connor's design, *The Lincoln of the Farewell Address,* received the commission.

Robert B. Atwood's article in the Worcester Sunday Telegram of 1934 reads: "Seventy three years ago today, Abraham Lincoln, a prairie lawyer who had been elected President of the United States, jolted in a hotel stage along the muddy streets of Springfield, Illinois. Without ceremony he was going to the railroad station, bound for the White House. It was eight o'clock in the morning of February 11, 1861. Rain and sleet sharpened the cutting edge of a raw wind, and made the weather disagreeable.

"At the station were a few friends buttoned against the elements who gathered to bid farewell to their neighbor. Lincoln mounted the rear platform of the train. He was pale with emotion, and obviously under a great strain. It had been said that he had a premonition that he was never again to set foot on Springfield ground, and that he was leaving forever the people he knew so well.

"The President-elect had prepared no speech for delivery at this time, but circumstances made one appropriate. His long figure tilted forward and his head bowed slightly as he looked down at his friends. His frock coat hung open, his arms were limp at his sides. With his features showing a serious appreciation of the task before him, Lincoln spoke."

He expressed himself with so much feeling, that the people who had gathered before him folded their umbrellas to see and hear more clearly what he had to say. They all knew instinctively that this was a very special occasion:

" My friends; no one, not in my situation can appreciate my feeling of sadness at this parting. To this place, and the kindness of these people, I owe everything. Here I have lived a quarter of a century, and have passed from a young to an old man. Here my children have been born, and one is buried. I now leave, not knowing when or whether I may return, with a task before me greater than that which rested upon Washington.

"Without the assistance of the Divine Being who ever attended him, I cannot succeed. With that assistance, I cannot fail. Trusting in Him who can go with me and remain with you, and be everywhere for good, let us confidently hope that all will yet be well. To His care commending you, as I hope in your prayers you will commend me, I bid you an affectionate farewell."

O'Connor, who had always admired Lincoln, took three years to finish the statue. It was truly a labor of love. Before he started, O'Connor read all of the biographies of Lincoln he could find, went to Springfield to study the site of the farewell address and studied the proposed setting for the statue and the approach to the Capitol building.

While in Lincoln's home town, O'Connor met people who remembered him as a neighbor. From Henry B.Rankin he secured a first-hand account of the farewell address. Rankin, author of *Personal Recollections of Abraham Lincoln* was one of the people who waited in the rain to bid Lincoln goodbye.

With this information in hand, O'Connor was ready to work. First he molded in clay a head of Lincoln about 18 inches tall. From this he made a plaster cast which stood at his side while he perfected the larger head that would be on the final statue.

Then followed the modeling of the body in clay, concentrating on the hands. Andrew thought Lincoln's hands were

Abraham Lincoln Facial Mask.
Permission Holy Cross College.
Worcester, MA.

beautiful - plain, angular, and humbly simple. He worked from the hand molds he had borrowed from Robert Todd Lincoln when he was in Springfield. Originally, when casting these hand molds, a problem arose. On the day the molds were to be cast, Lincoln had spent hours shaking hands with his well wishers, causing both hands to swell. The decision was quickly made that he should grasp something in his fists to disguise the swelling. After a quick search, a broom handle was found for him to grasp and the molds were then made. O'Connor was somehow able to sculpt the long angular hands of the President from these clenched fisted molds. It was fortunate for O'Connor that he met Robert Todd Lincoln, for not only the hands, but the facial masks were loaned to him. They had been cast by Leonard Volk, a sculptor from Wellstown, New York. He was first cousin of Mrs. Stephen Douglas. Born in 1828, he was close to ninety years old when Andrew met him. He had sculpted Douglas and done masks of both Douglas and Lincoln almost fifty five years before.

When the statue began to take shape, Robert Todd Lincoln came to Paxton and stayed for three days with the O'Connors. He went to the studio with Andrew in the morning, and visited with him all day watching as he worked. He approved thoroughly of Andrew's rendition of his father. Before he left, the facial masks and hand molds were given to O'Connor.

Six copies of the masks had been produced by Volk, and O'Connor obtained permission from him to do six more. One set was given to Daniel Chester French when he was commissioned to do the Lincoln Memorial in Washington, D.C., and one to Maurice Reidy, who donated it to Holy Cross College, Worcester, Massachusetts, where it is now on display in the archives.

Abraham Lincoln Hand Molds.
Permission Holy Cross College,
Worcester, MA.

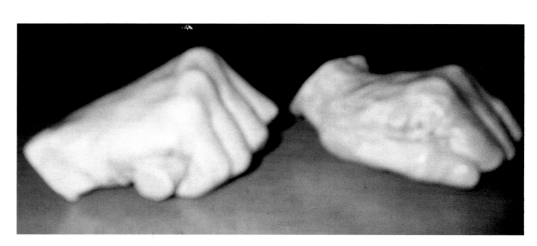

Seven commissioners from Illinois came at various times to view the statue while work was in progress. Many art lovers from Worcester thought that the "splendid statue of Lincoln was the finest thing of its kind ever made." Not only was the Abraham Lincoln a most satisfying experience for O'Connor, but the award for the contract was an impressive fifty thousand dollars.

Illinois celebrated the centennial of her admission to the sisterhood of states in 1918. On October fifth of that year the cornerstone of the Centennial Memorial Building was laid, and two statues of the citizens the state most desired to honor, were dedicated. Both of these statues stand before the state House between the walks leading to the East entrance. The statue of Lincoln stands at the beginning of the stairs leading from the street to the building, and fifty feet behind it, the statue of Stephen A. Douglas stands directly in front of the portico. From the street both statues are flanked by the colonnade and wings of the great building with its imposing dome rising 360 feet high in the air. Lincoln's speech is carved on the back of the large square of granite that represents the rear of the train on which he left Springfield.

There were always visitors to O'Connor's studio. Various commissioners came to view the progress of their particular monument. Jesse scheduled their calls for times when Andrew's work wouldn't be interrupted. Louis Sullivan, a good friend and famous architect whom O'Connor met at the Chicago Fair, came for a visit. He was determined to beat an alcohol problem, and was substituting chocolate for the alcohol he craved. Every day Jesse had to go to the local grocery store to buy chocolate for Louis. Sullivan was one of America's finest architects and designed and built the first skyscrapers. He was one of Frank Lloyd Wright's instructors. While he was at the Paxton studio, he spent every day with Andrew designing an idea of a war memorial for Washington, D.C. to be known as *The Arrival.* This memorial was produced with a staff mixture of plaster and straw and made into a very large, square slab. An ornate pattern on the front had a niche in which a young girl that O'Connor chose to name the *Virgin,* stood with a

Lincoln of the Farewell Address.
Standing before Springfield, Illinois
State Capitol.

76.

flower in her left hand. O'Connor incorporated the heads of Jesse and the four boys in this large monument.

Whatever Sullivan and O'Connor had in mind, *The Arrival* was never completed as modeled. The statue of the Virgin was presented to the Dublin Municipal Gallery in 1941, as well as the sculptures of the children's heads.

A week-long exhibit that Gertrude Whitney arranged in Newport in the summer of 1918 was ostensibly to sell some of O'Connor's work to the wealthy who summered there. It served as an introduction to another facet of her life that she wanted to share with him, and was an excellent excuse to see him again over a period of a week or two.

One can only imagine how awestruck Andrew was when he was ushered into the Breakers, the Vanderbilt summer cottage. The opulence and grandeur were greater than the grandest museums he had ever visited. His perception of this interesting woman that he loved, attained a new dimension, making him feel that the little he had done to help her career was not enough.

Gertrude must have enjoyed watching this country boy's surprise and wonder on seeing her mother's home The country's wealthiest people had summer cottages in Newport, affording a good market for Andrew's work. Gertrude now broached the subject of her impending commission for a monument to be placed in St. Nazaire, France. It was to honor the American soldiers who landed there in the War to aid the French in their fight. Of course he agreed. The only way that Andrew could show his appreciation for her generosity, was to help her become a famous sculptor.

The design she thought of, was an American eagle of colossal size with a wing spread of thirty feet. An American soldier stood in the center of its wings. Andrew knew that she couldn't possibly undertake this monument alone, and with little consideration of the moral aspects connected with it, urged her to pursue it. He already had a great amount of work in progress himself, this was just another burden.

78.

Gertrude was awarded the commission, and she and her assistant became very busy with the preliminary steps involved in sculpting a statue of such size.

Mrs. Whitney was to be commended for her war efforts from 1914 to 1918. Concerned with the victims of the war in France, she had established a hospital for wounded American and French soldiers. She spent the war years raising money to sustain its services, and frequently visited there. She certainly deserved the commission of a war memorial in that country.

In 1917 a group of commissioners came to Paxton from Glen View, Illinois, to speak to O'Connor Jr. about doing a statue to commemorate the patriotic work of the Boy Scout Movement. One of the members of their exclusive country and golf club, Edwin Stanton Jackman had left a bequest for this purpose. Theodore Roosevelt, who had been active in the Boy Scout movement, died at this time, so it was decided that the statue would also honor him. Consequently it became known as the *Boy Scout* or *Roosevelt Monument.*

O'Connor thought that this would be an opportunity to use his boys as models. Along with their dog Peggy, a small terrier, they took turns posing. The monument was placed at the head of a garden pool near the caddy shack on the grounds of the golf course. On the pedestal are three words symbolizing the Boy Scout spirit; "Youth, Life, Liberty."

Work on the memorial was begun in 1917 and it was unveiled in Glen View on July 4, 1919. The heads of the boys were exhibited as busts later. On a grander scale, just the heads, were incorporated into the O'Connor - Sullivan joint project, *The Arrival,* that they had enjoyed doing together.

The four years of war was over and people began to think about monuments in their public squares and parks to honor their war heroes. Soon after the Lincoln dedication a group from the city of Baltimore, Maryland approached O'Connor with a request that he sculpt an equestrian statue of General

Left: The Arrival composed of Staff material.
Never commissioned, a collaboration between
Louis Sullivan and O'Connor Jr.

LaFayette of Revolutionary War fame. Andrew was excited to be asked, remembering the Grant Equestrian he had worked on in the D.C. French studio. He had always wanted to do one on his own. French did not do horses, sending them out to be done by those who specialized in animals. O'Connor, however, wanted to do the whole statue and soon began. One can imagine how thrilled he was to tell his father about the latest commission. No doubt O'Connor Sr. visited the studio often as the horse was crafted and assembled. His expertise was probably needed many times in the crafting of the horse.

Marble sculpture does not long survive exposure to the American climate, while bronze weathers very well. Bronze acquires a rich patina as it ages. It offers much more versatility than marble and can be used for equestrian monuments very well. The legs of a rearing horse could not support the heavy mass of a marble or stone body. Very often in sculpting a figure, it was necessary to contrive some support in addition to the statue's legs. Tree trunks or some other device had to be worked into the design. A bronze figure, however, could stand alone, for the hollow torso posed no threat to the slenderness of the legs. A bronze equestrian monument could even be represented with the horse rearing on its hind legs.

Owen, O'Connor's oldest son modelled for the Marquis de LaFayette sculpture of the eighteen year old boy who came to America from France to help Washington fight the British in the Revolutionary War. O'Connor's work was not only a memorial to a distinguished French officer in the Colonial Army, but a monument to romance, beauty and vitality - to a love of liberty and the noble thoughts that animated this boy of the eighteenth century.

Owen spent many hours sitting on the back of Joe, the horse his father had bought to study the gait, mannerisms and muscles in movement. Owen rode back and forth on the driveway, galloping, stopping and walking. One can imagine what enjoyment the boys had with this new addition to the family. Andrew had to caution them not to hurt Joe, because he was a very valuable animal who had cost him twenty dollars. During the time he stayed with the O'Connor family,

Joe was probably kept busier than at any other time in his life, before or after.

In December, Gertrude arranged a one man exhibit for Andrew. The proceeds were to go to the Wharton War Charities. It was held in the Gallery of Jacques Seligman in New York City, which was, coincidently, next to the Whitney Gallery. Andrew made up a catalog of the work he was exhibiting and wrote the preface: "Were I a dweller in this great city I would no doubt be compelled by necessity to greater commercial effort. But living as I do in the remotest hills, my wants are few and sufficiently supplied without too great effort. It is not, therefore, a keen desire to sell my works which brings me here. Very likely it's vanity; but after somewhat more than twenty years of labor, the desire is strong to show my countrymen what I've made in all this time. Excepting the central porch of St. Bartholomew's Church and two works of less importance, none of my things has been seen in New York.

"My statue of Lincoln has appeared to me a sufficient

The Roosevelt or Boy Scout Monument. Permission of Glen View Country Club, Glen View, Illinois.

Marquis de LaFayette.
Washington Square,
Baltimore, MD.

excuse for holding this exhibition. Whatever I know or have learned is in this work; it is useless to look for religious or political meaning in it, there is none there.

"Simply from the mass of splendid material - masks, casts of his beautiful hands and numerous photographs - I've tried to take what I could use, to the end that I might show in sculpture, something of Lincoln's personal appearance.

"My forword has this virtue, at least, you'll be little fatigued by the reading, and for the rest, enter in and judge for yourselves.... Andrew O'Connor."

Gertrude had invited the O'Connor family to her home in New York City when the servicemen came home from the World War. Andrew, Jesse and the boys stood at the windows of the Fifth Avenue mansion and watched as the young men paraded before them. Patrick remember how impressed he was to be there. Andrew probably visited her home again during the Seligman exhibit. After setting up and arranging his works, he enjoyed the free time in New York with his friend. It was a legitimate excuse should anyone question their appearance together. Gertrude's Studio on MacDougal Alley was the gathering place of artists and friends of hers, and Andrew spent many pleasant hours there as well. A month in New York was a relaxing respite from the hard work of carving stone, and he undoubtedly enjoyed meeting the latest American artists who came to Gertrude's Gallery.

The Chicago Journal printed a review of the exhibit soon after it opened; "A very big personality is revealed by the works in the current exhibition.. Forty eight pieces of sculpture constituting a really important display, and giving the public a rare treat, for it is but seldom that one finds in New York an absolutely non-commercial art show. O'Connor's work is closely knit with the past and yet it is vitally of the present."

A different interpretation of the exhibit was put forth by the New York Times: "There is a serious note throughout, as though the sculptor has his mind continually in touch with the great human tragedy as he sees it enacted from year to year. Scarcely has he seen the lighter side of life, occupying himself with monumental single figures such as Lincoln and the Soldier of 1898, or compositions of largely religious inspiration. One of the latter, a small marble hewn in the rough block represents the weeping Magdalene at the feet of Christ on the Cross. The treatment of the Christ is most individual in its expression to the agony which convulses the body even after the soul has left it.

"This group and the despondent figure of Adam as he leaves the garden forever speak of the endless suffering of the race and seems to knit the present age of tragedy with those long past.
   "The sculptor's figure of Lincoln in a simple and characteristic standing pose is undoubtedly one of the most forceful statues of the martyred president yet conceived. It is unfortunate that it could not be shown here in bronze rather than the white plaster..."

In a letter to his friend Maurice Reidy from the Hotel Manhattan, New York, on the 25th of January 1918, Andrew wrote: "The exhibition, remaining open until the end of the month is doing pretty well, although the Metropolitan Museum bought only one head, a bronze for $2300.00.

"The former Miss Harriman bought the little Barry for $3000.00, and this is all the real money so far, that has changed hands."

He mentioned that the Pittsburgh Museum would be putting the exhibit on display for two months, beginning in April at their own expense and promising certain sales. He closed with; "The Metropolitan Museum opens an exhibit in two weeks and Mr. French has asked for four of my things, assuring me of at least one more sale there if I will send them, so I'm going to. I know you'd want to know about these things."

In the spring, Andrew was pleased to be elected an Associate of the National Academy of America - an honor from his own country that he appreciated.

In October and November of 1919, Andrew exhibited at the Luxembourg museum in Paris as a part of the "Exposition d'Artistes de l' Ecole Americain". A bronze statuette of John Barry and marble bust of Edward Tuck were both purchased by the Museum of Modern Art in Paris.

In July the Roosevelt memorial was unveiled at the Glen View Country Club in Chicago, and Hector, Owen, Roderick, Paddy, and Peggy the dog, will be forever young, standing at the head of the lily pool looking so vibrant that one almost expects them to move.

During a visit to New York that year, O'Connor was invited to lunch with some of his friends there. They discussed the adverse public portrait that had been painted of Stanford White after his murder, and wanted to stand and be counted as people who supported and loved him. Thus they planned a gift of memorial doors for the library at New York University in the Bronx. Thomas Hastings headed the executive committee, assisted by Thomas Dewing, Frederick MacMonnies, and several others among White's close friends. Lawrence Grant White was invited to design the pair of bronze doors - the eight panels were to be created by Herbert Adams, Philip Martiny, Andrew O'Connor, and Adolph Weinman. All of these artists had worked with Stanford White and wanted to honor the memory of a man who had endeared himself to many through his kindness and generosity.

Before the doors were installed, they were exhibited in the Fifth Avenue windows of the Gorham Company Building that White had designed and on which O'Connor had done sculptural decorating. At the dedication on December 10, 1921, Royal Cortissoz, who had worked at 57 Broadway many years before, gave the principle address. It was suggested that the doors were an especially appropriate memorial, since Stanford White himself had always been opening doors for others during his lifetime.

O'Connor exhibited the plaster model of his Roosevelt memorial at the Art Alliance in Philadelphia in 1920. An exhibit by the Society of Painters, Sculptors, and Gravers was put on for the first time in Buffalo, New York, where O'Connor exhibited his *Head of the Virgin* and *Fauness.* In his Paxton studio, he was doing final touch-ups on his equestrian and a bronze plaque honoring Orlando Whitney Norcross, to be placed in the Worcester City Hall, outside the Mayor's office.

Coincidentally, Andrew Sr. was finishing a bronze tablet dedicated to Alonzo Knapp Learned, a noted scholar and poet in the town of Holden. He attended the unveiling ceremony at the Damon Memorial Library of Holden, across the street from his home.

The O'Connor boys remembered the early 1920's in Paxton as the best times of their lives. Andrew Jr. was happily busy and his father had work, although he visited as often as possible, delighting in the fact that his son had become an important sculptor. It was a tedious trip from Holden to Worcester to Paxton by trolley car, and two miles by foot, so until Andrew Jr. bought a car, Sr. found it difficult to visit frequently. When the journey was a matter of thirty minutes, and he was being driven there, he was happy to go to Paxton whenever he had time to spare.

His own home was quiet now with only Cora and himself, and the noise and bustle of his son's house was pleasant to his ears.

Everyone in the young O'Connor family was kept busy. Each of the boys was given a quarter of the garden to weed and care for in the summer months. Aristide and Helene were in and out of the house and studio; he helping Andrew, and she visiting Jesse. Helene loved going through the studio, and kept watch on all the finished work. She had a great respect and love for Andrew.

Sometime in 1921, Helene received word from her parents in Paris that her brother had died, and she must come home. Money wasn't available for both she and Aristide to travel, and Aristide didn't want to go back, so Helene bid a tearful farewell to all of them and went home.

In 1920, Andrew Jr. exhibited the plaster model of his Roosevelt memorial at the Art Alliance of Philadelphia.

The International Peace Conference of 1899 led to the construction of a "Peace Palace" and the creation of a permanent Court of Arbitration at the Hague in the Netherlands in 1907. The Dutch had avoided involvement in World War I, fully believing that peaceful negotiations could solve world problems. In 1914 O'Connor won the bid for the commission to sculpt a statue to represent peace, to be placed in the central rotunda of the Hague Peace Palace. Once again his early molds of Jesse were used for the figures of the young women who would represent peace.

The statue, titled *Justice,* was a gift from the United States. The monument originally was comprised of two females, the one eventually erected, plus another that stood beside it with the right arm raised and the left hand touching the first on the shoulder. The design was ultimately changed to one female, petite and feminine. From this work came two plaster heads, one nineteen inches high and one normal size.

Gertrude came to visit the Paxton studio one summer. Her touring car was parked in the driveway, with the chauffeur standing beside it as she went inside to 'confer' with Andrew and view his latest work, which was the almost finished LaFayette. With great excitement, she asked Andrew if he would help her do an equestrian statue if she could obtain a commission. Andrew had enjoyed sculpting the first one and since it was almost completed, he agreed. Also, he did not have any other large commissions at this time.

From the kitchen Jesse could see the limousine and one can understand her feelings, when she told Owen she wished he could throw some glass under the tires. A small revenge for the pain she suffered from Gertrude Vanderbilt Whitney.

By 1922, Gertrude had bought a piece of land in Cody, Wyoming and accepted a commission from the the people of the city to sculpt a bronze statue of Buffalo Bill. Finished by 1924, the horse had more vitality and spirit than O'Connor's LaFayette. He had learned how to do a standing horse for the first monument, and was proficient enough to do one that looked as though it were about to rear up on its hind legs by the time he worked on Mrs. Whitney's. The figure of a young man in the Buffalo Bill statue is leaning to the left, scanning the ground with his right arm raised, carrying a rifle. Known as *The Scout,* it stands in Cody, Wyoming, on a raised platform of stone above the Shoshone River, facing the Eastern entrance of Yellowstone Park.

By 1923, one would have supposed that the *Justice* would have been put up in the Hague rotunda. Instead, as a letter to Father Earls from the Hotel Powhatan, Washington, D.C. on January 12, 1923, relates; "This is just to tell you I'm in Washington trying to get my statue for the Hague formally approved by the officials of the State Department, and am meeting with serious difficulty, with danger of coming to a break over the matter at any moment. I'm badly in need of aid from some person of influence in this stagnant root of incom petence. I'll probably be here another week, unless I'm thrown out sooner.
"Send me your blessing, Father, and accept my best wishes. P.S. Won't you telephone my wife a little word to cheer her up, it's not gay on that hill all alone in winter."

Andrew Sr.'s work in the early 1920's was a large funeral monument for Mathew Whittall of Worcester, who owned a carpet factory. At that time his fine wool carpets were known all over the country. The Whittall name became known as a symbol of carpet quality. He purchased his family burial plot high on a hill overlooking his factory. When he died, his family asked Andrew Sr. to design the monument to be chiseled from a large white limestone slab.

As the statue progressed, he came into the house after a day's work, very weary with an ache in his legs that never ceased. O'Connor Sr. was in his seventies and chiseling stone was grueling work. By the time he had finished the Whittall memorial, his legs were chronically painful.

Andrew Jr. had finished the *La Fayette* and Jesse wanted to get away from another Paxton winter, so they decided to go to Italy for six months. Andrew Jr. persuaded his father to come along with them, hoping that a winter in a warmer climate would help his legs feel better.

O'Connor Sr. could not leave until after Christmas, as Cora wanted to spend the holidays with the family. They arranged to meet in Genoa in January. O'Connor's daughter Adeline lived in Genoa and he was anxious to visit with her.

Andrew Jr. and his family were gone and his father and Cora were to leave from Boston on the White Star Liner "Arabic". In an article submitted to the Worcester Telegram O'Connor Sr. wrote; "The ship was manned by Italians, carrying Italians and bound for the city at which we wished to land.

"Thus it happened that on the day and hour upon which the vessel was to sail from Boston, we found ourselves among a numerous gathering of the sons and daughters of Italy, who like ourselves, were waiting its arrival from New York.

"But the hour passed without our impatient eyes seeing signs of its coming, and then another hour was announced from a distant belfry, and still no ship flying the flag of Italy."

Whittall Memorial.
Hope Cemetery,
Worcester, MA.

O'Connor at work in his studio on Adam and Eve.

"Finally word came that the ship's progress had been delayed by a heavy fog. while en-route from New York. Fortunately for the waiting men, women and children, the air that played around them in the huge barnlike structure was that of September, for had it been the biting cold of December, they would certainly have suffered. There was no means in sight for heating the building and no where to sit." An amenity sorely missed by one whose legs ached so interminably. The ship, having been held up by fog, finally arrived, and about eleven in the morning all the passengers and their baggage were on board. Andrew Sr. enjoyed the voyage despite the fact that there were only twenty two people in first class who spoke English well. This was on a part of the ship designed to hold hundreds. Travel to Europe in the 1920's had begun to decline, and the steamship companies were selling their ships at auction for a fraction of their worth. A week later, the elder O'Connors met the rest of the family in Genoa.

In a letter to Father Earls on January 29th, 1924 Andrew Jr. complained; "It's perhaps just as well we escaped the winter in Worcester, but winter in Rome forces the stranger to wear his warmest clothing - especially indoors. No warmth is to be found anywhere except in the most expensive hotels. Hector is enchanted, in spite of all inconveniences - but the rest of us suffer too much material discomfort to enjoy as we should - the beautiful things all around. It's with a kind of joy that I look forward to our return home. We are now in Florence where we intend to stay until the middle of March, but my wife is not happy here, and I, when I'm not in the galleries or churches, am lost in a city utterly foreign to all my tastes.

"Paddy works in the Uffizze Gallery and Roderic is always busy, but we all look forward to seeing you again this summer."

They had not been in Italy long when O'Connor Sr. began feeling poorly. With deep concern over his father's health, Andrew suggested that perhaps he would feel better in Paris. He had been approached to judge the summer Olympic Games which were to take place in France. In a March 9th. letter from Florence, he explained why he had been appointed. "I'm sorry that in the departments of Literature and Music no Americans

90.

were sufficiently known to the French to receive the required number of votes - but in sculpture we have two members - MacMonnies and myself - and in painting, two. From Paris we go to the Hague and then home. I had hoped to stop in Ireland for a month, but I am so uneasy and desperately anxious to get to work that I must put this aside for another year. Anyway, we are all looking forward to seeing you again before very long. With all our best wishes."

O'Connor Sr.'s health only worsened during the three months they spent in Paris. In early June, he and his wife returned to Holden, his legs completely paralyzed. He was also suffering considerable pain. In April, Andrew Jr had wanted to go home, but as his father became progressively more ill, he dreaded the thought of returning if that meant he would lose him. As long as he remained in Europe, he was - supposedly, postponing what he knew and could not admit to himself - was inevitable.

On July 22, 1924 Andrew O'Connor Sr. died of paralysis at his home in Holden, Massachusetts. He was seventy eight years old. He had been home from his European trip for almost six weeks. At the time of his return, he was paralyzed below the waist and did not leave his bed after. The funeral of the senior O'Connor was from the Holden Congregational Church and burial in Hope Cemetery next to Mary Ella.

Crucifix.
Holy Cross College Library
Worcester, Massachusetts.

Andrew Jr. and his family returned for the funeral. Plans to get back to work in Paxton, immediately changed after the death of his father. The house and studio were put on the market and sold. All of their belongings were disposed of or packed, and before long, the studio was cleaned out and his work ready to be shipped to France. Andrew felt the way he had at fifteen when Mary Ella died, like a boat whose anchor had been severed and was left to drift. Paxton meant nothing to him without his father.

As a fond tribute to Father Earls, Andrew finished the statue of the *Crucifixion*. On the presentation of it, he said; "I have a great affection for my friends at Holy Cross, and give them this marble because I thought they would like to have it."

The diminutive statue presents a carved figure of Christ upon the cross with the sorrowing Madonna kneeling at his side. This piece joined the bust of Reverend Patrick T. O'Reilly that his father had sculpted - in the entrance to the Holy Cross Library.

At the time of O'Connor's presentation of his tribute in marble to his friend, Father Earls composed a five stanza poem, using the carved figures and O'Connor's recent bereavement as his subject he called it *Defeat of Sorrow*. The final verse reads:

> *"Sorrow cannot take you*
> *With his gold or dross*
> *Or his gloom of faces*
> *Dreading gain or loss,*
> *For you know sure peace*
> *Underneath the Cross."*

Father Earls understood how grief stricken Andrew was, though he didn't show it. He had denied the idea that his father was so ill, and had trouble facing the fact that he would no longer be there for him. They had become so close in the past ten years, he would feel a large vacancy in his life.

Maurice Reidy wrote about O'Connor's Crucifix; "Christ's body hangs by the nails and nothing else. So convincing is this effect that the figure would surely fall if these stone nails were removed...The Rodin influlence is here, strongly; the figure of Christ is grotesque. The body is painfully thin and bony, the hands are lifeless....The same shielding effect is made by the background stone as in ....*Maternity*. The technique is effective in making the figure of Christ seem lifeless and still, but the background gives the figure immense power."

In September of 1924, a special dispatch to the Worcester Telegram and Gazette from Baltimore, Maryland read:
   "The statue of Marquis de LaFayette by Andrew O'Connor of Worcester will be unveiled tomorrow and dedicated by President Coolidge. In this period of transition to another country, it is doubtful that Andrew Jr. found the time to attend this dedication.

Right:

Andrew O'Connor Sr. Funeral Monument. Picture by permission of D.C. French museum, Chesterwood.

There was one last painful task that Andrew had to perform before he could wind up his business in Paxton. He had to make the funeral monument for his father. The base he chose was a plain block of red granite with the words "In Memoriam" carved into the front. Attached to the base and extending to an overall height of six or seven feet, was attached a carved bronze plaque. While the clay was still wet, the four grandsons were called into the studio and asked to place their hands on it as a final gesture of respect for one they all loved.

Delorme Memorial.
Notre Dame Cemetery
Worcester, MA.

Iver Johnson Memorial
Hope Cemetery,'
Worcester, MA.

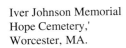

94.

VII

Paris Revisited

In 1925 the Paxton house, studio and land was quickly sold. Andrew and Jesse sadly packed up belongings, sculptures in progress, and family accoutrements, to move. Again it would be as far away from his pain as he could go, to Europe. His helper, Aristide, who liked the United States, chose to remain in the area where he had put down roots.

As they drove down the long driveway toward the state highway for the last time, their hearts were heavy. Andrew had looked forward to coming home and getting to work, all of the time he was in Europe. Now that the steadying light of his life had gone out, all he could think of was to flee. He was to spend the remaining years of his life in pursuit of work and happiness in places other than the United States. The most satisfying part of his life was over.

A large block of marble was left next to the stone wall at the gates of his property, awaiting the vehicle that would transport it abroad. For some months afterward, travelers coming up the dark highway at night were startled as they neared the driveway and the ghostly white marble apparition loomed before them. At that time the highway was not well travelled and there were many long stretches of forest and farm lands along the winding road to the town proper.

Both of the Andrew O'Connors were now gone from the city that loved them and was proud to declare them natives. They were not forgotten, however, as long as one of their statues or paintings was unveiled or an honor bestowed upon them anywhere in the world.

When the O'Connors returned to Paris in 1926, they rented a house on 17 Rue Champagne Premier. On June 5 Andrew and Gertrude went to the Salon together. He was exhibiting the Triple Cross that she thought "very impressive", although it was still in plaster. He also had his Commodore Barry in the exhibit.

Gertrude was exhibiting the plaster of her St. Nazaire eagle, thirty feet high with a wing-spread of thirty feet. Between the wings of the bird, stood the American soldier in uniform. This was to be placed near the ocean in the port city of St. Nazaire, France, where the American army first came ashore in World War I to aid the French against the German invaders.

During that summer in Paris, Andrew sent two cables to Gertrude in New York in regard to the war memorial commissioned for St. Nazaire. The first simply advised her that the memorial must be approved by the American Battle Monuments Commission, and the second stated that such approval was certain. Gertrude, however, ran into bureaucratic problems. In October, she was asked to make changes on the design. She refused, and after applying to many different governmental bureaucracies, appealed to President Coolidge for the permission she needed from the United States.

A small marble bust that O'Connor sculpted in 1923 bacame a part of our national heritage when it found a home in the White House. It had not been crafted for that purpose, however. Gertrude may have given the little marble called

Fortunata to the President to sweeten the request for the erection of the St. Nazairre monument

Still in the White House collection, it was used in the oval office during the Coolidge Administration and put into an adjacent drawing room during the Hoover and Roosevelt Presidencies. Eleanor Roosevelt had her picture taken with the statue at one time. In the nineteen fifties and sixties, it found itself in the Social Office of the East Wing. Since nineteen seventy one *Fortunata* has been in storage at times, and other times in the office of the curator. This small bust is twelve inches high with the head six inches wide and five and seven eighths inches deep.

By the end of 1926, Gertrude began plans for an elaborate unveiling ceremony in St. Nazaire for June of 1927. She was moving the finish date forward once again, pressuring Andrew to get it to the foundry for bronzing. This St. Nazaire statue, called atrocious and lacking merit, was condemned by many critics in the art community in New York.

On turning fifty years of age, Gertrude accompanied her mother to Europe for a month and a half. When she wasn't with her mother, she was spending her time with Andrew, who was overseeing the casting of sections of the huge St. Nazaire sculpture. She often went with him to the foundry.

All her thoughts were now centered on the St. Nazaire unveiling. There was always something that Gertrude needed to discuss with Andrew. They met for meals - where the questions of payments to workers were answered, commissions discussed, and whether she should consider them or not. Obviously they enjoyed being together, and monuments were the cement that bonded them.

Among works of three thousand exhibitors at the spring Salon in Paris at the Grande Palais, the plaster model of the soldier and eagle towered over every other sculpture exhibited.
St. Nazaire had received by far the greatest attention in the press. The monument was to be dedicated on June 26, 1926,

nine years after the American soldiers landed there under General John J.Pershing.

On June 25th, Gertrude, Andrew and thirty-four others took a special train to St.Nazaire. Thirty thousand people from the region attended the unveiling. All the houses and public buildings in the town displayed French and American flags. Festivities began with a parade of French and American Militiamen, followed by a twenty one gun salute as ships from both countries came into the harbor and ran up their colors. The crowd sang *The Marseillaise* and as the monument was unveiled, one hundred carrier pigeons with small French and American flags attached to them, were released from their cages and soared out to sea. Aerial bombs that burst into red, white and blue paper streamers spun through the air.

When the speeches began, Gertrude was made a Chevalier of the Legion of Honor by the Minister of the Marine. Concerts filled the afternoon, and fireworks lit the night. The celebration went on day after day, for many weeks. The news of it was carried by the major media world wide. Testimonial dinners were given for Gertrude with praise for her patriotism and efforts at international detente. She blossomed with all the wonderful compliments and attention for this was the part of sculpting that Mrs. Whitney loved best.

After the O'Connors returned to Paris in 1925, it wasn't long before Helene came to visit. No longer interested in Aristide, she had married a man named Desmairoux. Jesse was happy to see her again, and Helene resumed her research on Andrew's work, taking pictures and asking questions. When she thought she had enough material for her book, Helene's father, a newspaper publisher, printed and published it for her. The Helene Desmairoux book was called "L'Ouvre du Sculpteur O'Connor," (The Works of the Sculptor O'Connor.) It was very well done and the only book about Andrew's work that has been written. Andrew had thought over all the years that nothing would ever come of Helene's hobby until she arrived at the door one day in 1927 with the book in her hand. He couldn't believe that she had put it all together. He was impressed and flattered. After reading it, he packaged and sent a copy to Father Earls sharing his pleasure and expecting a favorable comment on it.

Accompanying the book was a letter: "At last a book - of which I've heard rumors for years - has appeared and I am sending you one of the earliest copies hoping you will accept it, and maybe - even like it.

"We have no hope of seeing you for a good while - unless you'll come over here - for I am occupied in Spain for at least another year - and then for some time in England. The others are all working hard and doing admirable work."

Probably one of the subjects that Andrew had engaged upon in his conversations with Gertrude, was his fascination with La Rabida, the monastery that he knew from the Chicago Fair, and the impression it had made upon him. Gertrude began thinking about it, and took a motor trip to Spain with a side trip to Huelva and Palos and La Rabida Monastery. During this trip she formulated the idea of a monument to *Columbus*. When she returned home, she presented the plan to Andrew. She knew that he had always wanted to build a heroic statue, so why not do it in Spain, the place from which Columbus had sailed. The idea was beyond anything either of them had ever thought about, but as they discussed it, the excitement for the project grew, and finally, with Andrew's blessing, Gertrude began to speak to her wealthy friends about funding.

In August of 1926, Gertrude received a letter from a Wall Street lawyer friend named William H. Page. In it, he proposed that if she were considering doing a statue of Columbus in Spain similar to the size and scope of St. Nazairre, he was interested. He would get sponsorship and contributions from the Knights of Columbus, for a Columbus Memorial fund that would accept donations for the project. Page appointed Alexander P. Moore, former ambassador to Spain as the president of the Columbus Memorial Fund. Moore, however, was not a good choice, and caused much controversy, pitting the towns of Huelva and Palos, proposed sites for the statue, against each other. Furthermore, he insulted several Spanish aristocrats and clashed with the Spanish Monarchy regarding the final spot for the monument.

To smooth things, Gertrude spent three months in Spain. She met many times with the Duke of Alba, and finally had him arrange an audience with King Alfonso. She and the king agreed on the Town of Huelva. Moore, of course, wanted Palos. Finally, after much maneuvering, Gertrude had Moore replaced and Huelva was the chosen site.

In March when Gertrude came to Paris, Andrew joined Gertrude at her studio late in the afternoon of March eleventh. As at all their reunions, there was much to talk about. He was very interested in her design of *Columbus*, and suggested they provide an opening in the top of the statue to let a beam of light fall on the two statues to be placed inside the pedestal.

In the United States, the Boston Sunday Post of March 20, 1927, reported; "Andrew O'Connor has just been invited to go to Angora (Ankara) to make a statue of Mustapha Kemal. The Turkish government wants a huge figure of Kemal on horseback to be placed in front of the parliament building in the new capitol." O'Connor was chosen to create the statue after studying the work of all the sculptors in Europe and the invitation to come to Angora was a very great tribute to his work. Following the execution of the statue, there was however, no information available as to the outcome of it or what it looked like.

On March 22, Gertrude arrived back in Paris and immediately went to Andrew's studio. He was returning to the States the next day, and again there were many hours of discussion. They spent the day together and she then gave him her preliminary sketch of the *Columbus* monument to take to New York for enlargement.

When he returned to Paris, Gertrude persuaded Andrew to go with her to Huelva and confirm the place she had picked, before she purchased it. O'Connor approved the site she had chosen next to the shore. Since they were staying several days, they used a room at a local establishment, and after touring the surrounding countryside and visiting La Rabida, Andrew left to go back to Paris. Gertrude remained to purchase the property and finalize all the details with Huelva officials.

She was proficient in these skills and enjoyed this part of the preparation as much as the finish celebrations.

Gertrude designed a colossal figure of *Columbus*, about fifty to seventy five feet high. His arms would be resting on a cross. He was to stand on a rectangular pedestal about half the height of the figure, with bronze bas reliefs representing the four hemispheres on each of the four upper corners. Inside the pedestal, the seated statues of Queen Isabella and King Ferdinand would be designed and executed by Gertrude. O'Connor visited her studio twice in the spring to go over details of the statue, and on the evening of July 1, O'Connor had dinner with her. Never enough time together, they met again the following day for lunch and then visited the Salon. The Exhibit was over and cleaned out except for a few large pieces.

Gertrude began the Ferdinand and Isabella sometime in June, and had them ready for casting by August 20, with little time for social life, except an occasional dinner out with Andrew or another male friend. O'Connor was so busy with his own work and the constant traveling to Spain to direct the work-men, he did not have time to help Mrs. Whitney with the statues that would be placed in the base

Between his visits to Spain, Andrew was working on a statue of Tristan and Iseult, the hero and heroine of the Arthurian legend of the prince who fell in love with the Irish princess Iseult and died with her. Carving the marble statue was a welcome relief from the exhausting work involved in building the Columbus of a fifty foot or more height.

In June, Andrew wrote to Maurice Reidy in Worcester, thanking him for a loan that Hector had repaid for him. He mentioned that Hector was now second secretary for the American Delegation Conference for the Limitations of Naval Armament at Geneva. He also wrote that Roderic and Paddy had the best oil paintings in the Salon of 1927.

At the Salon of 1928, Andrew exhibited his *Tristan and Iseult,* while in his studio, he worked on a statue called *Ghosts.* The

102.   Fortunata. Property of the White House.
Washington, D.C.

Judges at the 1928 Spring Salon were so impressed with the Tristan and Iseult that they awarded O'Connor their gold medal. This made Andrew O'Connor the first foreigner to be so honored by the Society of French Artists. He was enormously proud of the honor bestowed upon him.

During one of their conversations, Gertrude mentioned that St. Patrick's Cathedral in New York City would be given new doors by an anonymous donor. She knew he loved doing doors, and Andrew became very excited about the prospect of something as prestigious as St. Patrick's Cathedral. Not only would he be doing them for the money but for the joy of working in New York once again.

Andrew immediately wrote to Father Earls on September 20, 1928. "I want to..ask you for your help. Mr. George McDonald of New York proposes to offer some bronze doors for the central porches of St. Patrick's Cathedral to Archbishop Hayes. I wish he would employ me to make them, and considering my past performances - such as the doorway of St. Bartholomew's, New York - perhaps I am the most qualified to do this work."

He went on to say that he had reason to believe that a decision was imminent as to who was to do the work. He was prevailing on their friendship and the importance of Father Earls' influence in the Church, to recommend him for the commission. In a post-script he mentioned that he had just returned to Paris from Dublin where he and Jesse had spent six of the happiest weeks of his life.

The *Columbus* monument was taking shape and Gertrude, anxious to see the progress, pressed Andrew to tell her when it would be a good time for her to go to Spain. In mid-October, he sent her a telegram in New York telling her that it was not necessary for her to come. It was a long, tedious journey and he wished to spare her the long train ride. Things were going along very well. The stone pedestal was almost finished. The statue should be ready to mount in December. He had twenty men working on it. The bronze bas reliefs were finished and would be set in the pedestal by October 26th. The stone interior of the pedestal was being completed in Paris and would be ready by January 1929. He reported that the rough stone seawall - needed to protect the statue against high seas, was now in place, and added that he would be in Huelva the following week adjusting stone panels. He asked her to please send thirty thousand dollars immediately - to be paid to the contractor.

Gertrude was doing all the negotiating and paper work with the commissioners - as well as paying the help. She was unique. There were no artisans of any kind who could do business the way she did. She was able to get commissions that others couldn't. Because O'Connor was doing the work, the commissioners knew they were getting a good job and she was reliable about finishing and paying for the work at the stipulated time.

If there wasn't money immediately available, she had enough personally to cover bills temporarily. O'Connor however, had to work at a faster rate than he desired, and to a stressful deadline. It was becoming difficult for their romance to survive a demanding employer-employee relationship. No wonder Andrew was so happy during his six weeks in Ireland with an uncomplicated Jesse.

While O'Connor was busy on *Columbus*, Gertrude was negotiating more work. A monument was being considered for Springfield, Massachusetts. Gertrude wanted to use the soldier on the bier, designed for the "Debarquement" group. A gruesome statue that she proposed to soften by placing a mother holding a child, beside it. Gertrude wanted to use the soldier in some fashion, however the Commissioners procrastinated for several years, and then dropped the idea as money became very tight with the onset of the Depression.

On November 7, 1928, O'Connor wrote to Father Earls: "Your kindly efforts caused the architect, Mr. George McDonald to send me the necessary information regarding the doors for St. Patrick's, but curiously enough it is your friend Mr. Maginnis of Boston - architect of your college, who

104.

is the adviser touching all this new work on the Cathedral. Will you write to him about it?"

In his last letter, Father Earls had mentioned that the Archbishop of Baltimore had criticized O'Connor's work ethics, perhaps concerning his association with Gertrude. His reply to Father Earls was testy: "I'm sorry the Archbishop of Baltimore has a poor opinion of my manner of work, but there are evil persons in America who exert themselves to make my path as difficult as possible-and I dare say his Grace has been told I'm stubborn." Once brought to his attention, no doubt the fact that Father Earls questioned what he was doing, gnawed on his mind as he worked the long hours in Spain. As the deadline for the unveiling approached, the stress became unbearable.

Knowing that it was near completion, Gertrude finally decided that she should see the *Columbus*. O'Connor had returned to Paris before she went to Huelva with her daughter Flora. She stayed in the small, uncomfortable rented room accessible only through the town's largest restaurant, that she had shared with Andrew at the beginning of the project. One had to walk the length of the restaurant and up some stairs in the rear to reach the drab accommodations. The walls were ugly, the furniture was second hand castoffs, and the carpet worn, but here, she and Andrew could be together without any question. Flora could not understand why her mother would pick such a place to stay but Gertrude had no complaints about it, seeming not to notice how depressing the room was.

In a telegram from Huelva to O'Connor in Paris, she wrote: "EVERY MAN TURNED UP THIS MORNING ON HIS JOB INCLUDING ME. HOPE FOR SAME TOMORROW. THREE CARLOADS STONE DELIVERED. THREE MORE AT STATION. CHANCES SCAFFOLD WILL BE DOWN END THIS WEEK. MCAULLIFFE OUT TODAY, MISS YOU...BUT PLEASE DON'T HURRY BACK."

F.J. McAulliffe was the sculptor that O'Connor hired as an assistant when he couldn't be there.

In her diary, Gertrude wrote that the fatigue she had suffered in the beginning of the *Columbus* affair must have been because of the emotional ties to this huge monument. Now however, "To see suddenly before you the real dream in great blocks of stone is overpowering..." She continued that at first the work involved mundane things, such as who to get to work on the project - how many men would be needed - how much stone, etc., but now she wrote: "God, the fascination of building, of creation - and always back of it the dream come true - the vision materialized."

The unveiling of the *Columbus* and the preparations for it took months of Gertrude's time, but this was the part of the process she enjoyed most of all. She wrote invitations to all her friends including the Spanish Duke of Alba. Gertrude planned to transport her friends to Huelva in a private train from Paris to Seville, with a day's layover at the Ritz in Madrid; then by a chartered cruise ship from Seville, down the Guadalquivir River, and along the Spanish coast to Huelva.

The great day arrived and *Columbus* was ready to be unveiled. The guests had partied all the way from Paris on her private train. During the two day layover at the Madrid Ritz, some of her friends went to the bullfights and others enjoyed the sights. As the cruise ship sailed down the river they partied. Cecil Howard played the guitar and improvised songs about his fellow passengers and the sights they saw on the banks as they cruised by.

For all the passengers, one small incident remained in their memory. The night before reaching Huelva, one or more persons roamed through the ship, tying all of the men's pajamas in knots, and soaking all of them - including the Duke of Alba's! The Duke was enraged. Everyone had theories as to who did the dastardly deed, and of course Gertrude's socialite friends blamed her artist friends. Nevertheless, everyone was still laughing about the pajama scandal when the boat reached Huelva.

Jesse was worried about Andrew's health in the final phase of the project. He was becoming increasingly tired and pale.

Patrick was living in Paris, and frequently came home to see them. On Jesse's request, he took a train to Spain to help his father finish the huge monument. He remembered on the day of the dedication, how he and his father stood waiting at the monument with everyone who was not 'inner-circle.' There was a cold, dreary rain falling. The time came and went for the unveiling. Finally, the cruise ship came into view. No doubt the sight of the ship with all Gertrude's famous friends laughing and talking, brought the truth home to Andrew. He would never be any more to Mrs. Whitney than a vehicle to promote her own career and fame. He had enjoyed her happiness when the Arlington fountain was unveiled, with its attending publicity, and probably had some misgivings when the St. Nazaire statue was unveiled accompanied by so much hooplah. Suddenly however, he saw all the hypocrisy of what he had been doing for Gertrude - through his love for her, the waste of so much time given to her works that he might have legitimately used on his own.

Long before, D.C. French had tried to warn him of his folly as did his own contemporaries on MacDougal Alley. Perhaps the one who really opened his eyes was his best friend, Father Earls. He cared so much, and tried to influence Andrew by relating his recent conversation with the Archbishop.

No one could have felt more alone. Andrew in his exhaustion, had caught typhoid fever. After all the speeches were made, and everyone had enjoyed a lavish luncheon in the huge tents set up for the celebration, Gertrude and her guests returned to the cruise ship for more festivities. All the people of Huelva and surrounding areas returned to their homes. Andrew and Patrick were left to pack up the tools and climb on a train for Paris where Andrew immediately checked into the hospital. During his three weeks there, Andrew had ample time to think about his life and where it was headed. He was no longer young and reckless and had to think about his future. He realized that he didn't have the strength to continue working as he had.

There is no known record of his conversation with Gertrude following the Huelva unveiling. Perhaps he simply told her that he would not be a party to this arrangement any longer.

Gertrude had commissions in the works, but knew that without Andrew's help, she could never complete them - a sudden letdown from the elation she had been experiencing for so many years. She had taken for granted that this collaboration would go on forever.

No-one ever dissolved a relationship with Gertrude Whitney.....When she tired of them she dropped them completely, but she had never experienced anyone tiring of her, and she must have been very angry and hurt. After all the publicity and excitement that the *Columbus* had generated, this was an enormous letdown.

Columbus Monument.
Huelva Spain.
Permission of:
Flora Miller Irving.
Whitney Museum.

VIII

Life after Gertrude

Some time after his experience in Spain, O'Connor was able to face the truth and rationalize it enough to write to Father Earls: "I've finally got done with my job in Spain, and am happy to be free from what was a trying and difficult work, and to be able to get along again with my own affairs. I've been in Spain about 15 times in the last year and a half now; if God is good to me, I shall never see that country again."

He mentioned that the Salon was open again, and that Roderic and Paddy were exhibiting excellent pictures. As usual he was never free from thoughts of the St. Patrick's doors and wrote: "I've never heard any more about the bronze doors... except that some Jews were getting baptized - in the hope they'd get the work as being good Catholics. I wonder who will be chosen. I hope it will be me."

Two weeks later on May 31, 1929, he apparently had good news from Father Earls, because he answered: "I sent you a cable as soon as I received your confidential letter, and I'm hoping that at last the Church will give me a chance to make the best doors in the world." He then admitted to Father Earls that he had been offered the chance to do the main doors for the Cathedral of St. John the Divine a year ago, but didn't accept the offer, even though there was more money involved than the St Patrick's doors would bring him. He wrote that he wasn't interested in doing the St. John the Divine doors; but, in fact, he was too busy with the *Columbus* to do anything else.

O'Connor's letter continued with the information that the Salon was now open, and he enclosed a photograph of the fragment of a monument to the War that he was exhibiting. The statue was probably the *Mother of Sorrows*. The greatest benefit derived from exhibiting in the Salon was the exposure to potential customers.

It was not long before The Worcester Telegram published another news story concerning Andrew at this time: "Native of Worcester, Andrew O'Connor sculptor, has again received foreign acclaim and honor, this time one never before accorded an American.

"With honors from the United States and Europe already placing him among the great masters of the world, Andrew O'Connor again brings recognition to his native land as the only American sculptor represented in the National Gallery in London. *Mother of Sorrows* his newest work of sculpture, a bronze figure...of a woman has been accepted for permanent exhibition in the Tate Gallery in London...Although it is acknowledged a complete artistic conception, it is but a replica of part of a great war memorial planned by O'Connor for erection in the United States. A kneeling figure not yet bronzed, and a wounded soldier already in the museum will have a place in the completed carving." The three fragments of the *Debarquement* had finally found a home after ten years of uncertainty.

In his studio, O'Connor was working on a seated Lincoln, a Lincoln bust for London, and several smaller busts of Lincoln. Some of his Lincolns were carved from sandstone and some bronzed.

1929 was a memorable year in O'Connor's life. It was at this time that the government of France bestowed upon him the

Chevalleur of the Legion d'Honneur, a great honor for a foreigner to receive.

An October 1st. letter to Father Earls mentioned his Spanish work once again. "My last voyage in Spain was one too many and I came out with typhoid, which has caused me great loss of time for three months past; but to have worked for 15 months beside La Rabida Convent where Columbus passed his last night in Spain before sailing on his great voyage, and to have been intimately associated with Brother Leon, the present head of the convent, and to see what he is in the midst of a corrupt society, was, I dare say, compensation for all I suffered, and God knows I was never so tried by the almost insurmountable difficulties I had to contend against.

"In spite of all, I built the monument, taught the natives.. how to work and carried through the affair, and when President de Rivera came to inaugurate it, everything was finished, and I came back to Paris"... (This letter was meant to be confidential, for Fr. Earls only.)

Turning the subject once again to the doors, he thanked Father Earls for his help and the note from Mr. Maginnis: "I am very anxious to do that work, for I'm now at the age when I must do my best work, or not at all. I'll finish the Lincoln for Providence in two or three months, and then I'd like to begin the doors."

Andrew didn't think to tell Father Earls that this was to be kept confidential, so on receiving this letter, Father Earls was pleased to tell the press that O'Connor had once again done a wonderful statue. This time it was of Columbus, located in Spain.

As news travels rapidly, it is almost certain that Gertrude became informed that O'Connor was telling the world that she did not sculpt the Columbus. This served to affect Gertrude much like a bear's paw in a nest of angry bees. The Columbus monument was not yet over for O'Connor...

On December 25, 1929, Andrew wrote a Christmas wish to Father Earls, thinking of him up on the hill where Holy Cross is located. He thought that probably the snow was deep and the winds fierce as they should be on Christmas Day. In France it was just wet and miserable, but not very cold. He hoped that Father Earls would like the seated Lincoln for Providence, Rhode Island. The work had been delayed by his illness and hospital stay of the past summer and the resultant exhaustion. Once again he mentioned, "I wonder whatever has become of the question of the doors for St. Patrick's. I never hear any more about them..."

On December 31, 1929, Father Earls received an urgent telegram from O'Connor: "AN INDIVIDUAL FROM THE BALKANS HAS HAD IT PUBLISHED IN NEW YORK PAPERS AS WELL AS HERE THAT HE HAS RECEIVED THE ORDER FOR SAINT PATRICK'S WORK, CAUSING IT TO BE UNDERSTOOD THAT HE HAS BEEN CHOSEN IN PREFERENCE TO ME. AM DEEPLY ANXIOUS TO KNOW IF THIS INJUSTICE HAS BEEN DONE ME. YOU ARE MY PATRON AND SO I APPEAL TO YOU. SHOULD I ENDEAVOR TO SEE THE CARDINAL HIMSELF BEFORE IRRETRIEVABLE ACTION IS TAKEN THAT WILL RUIN WHAT SHOULD BE AN INSPIRED AND INSPIRING WORK? FORGIVE ME AND ACCEPT SINCEREST BEST WISHES FOR THE NEW YEAR..."

St. Patrick's Cathedral
New York City, NY.

On receipt of this wire, Reverend Earls wired the architects for the project, Maginnis and Walsh, who responded promptly, on January 4, 1930. They maintained that there was no basis for the report unless Cardinal Hayes had acted while he was in Europe, which probably wasn't likely. They said that they were going to ask for a meeting with him when he returned.

On January 8, 1930, O'Connor sent a telegraph to Reverend Michael Earls at Holy Cross College. "BY INVITATION SIR GEORGE VISITED HIS EMINENCE, CARDINAL HAYES AND RECEIVED COMMAND TO BEGIN WORK. SIR GEORGE WISHED ME TO TELL YOU HIS ADMIRATIONS YOUR FRIENDSHIP AND LOYALTY." Sir George apparently referred to George Mc Donald, architect and emissary of Cardinal Hayes in Europe. In a following letter, he explained fully. A day or two after he had sent the cable about the Balkan sculptor, Sir George visited him in Paris. After hearing the story of the Balkan man, he took O'Connor back to San Remo with him, and had him speak to the Cardinal. His Eminence was as kind to O'Connor as Sir George had been. Fortunately, he had brought some designs with him. "His Eminence advised me - helped me and praised me, and I'm now working - with the fires burning bravely - on the Porch of the Holy Virgin - having drawn to scale the Porch of Christ."

Andrew was deeply touched by the kindness that Cardinal Hayes and Sir George had shown him. When he asked if he could write to Father Earls with the good news, they urged him to do so, as it was the fine friendship they shared that had caused all the good things to happen. He closed the letter to his friend with the promise that he would do great doors, and said he would be seeing him in April, as he had much to talk about.

On the fifteenth of January, the architect Maginnis sent a letter to Father Earls, telling him how pleased he was that O'Connor was finally doing the doors. He felt, however, that in the interest of time, all of the doors should not be given to him, but only the central ones, and O'Connor should consider himself very lucky to have such a friend in Worcester.

On the 29th of January, O'Connor wrote to Father Earls enclosing photographs of the seated Lincoln. Andrew wanted him to be the first to see them and comment on whether he liked them or not. He promised to be in New York in March.

By January 1930, the seated Lincoln was finished and ready to be bronzed at the Gorham foundry in Providence, Rhode Island. Since 1927 Andrew had worked on the commission to do a seated Lincoln for the State House of the City of Providence. His price of $20,000 had been accepted, to be paid by donations from the school children of Providence. The dedication was to be on Lincoln's birthday, 1931, and O'Connor worked toward that date.

When the delivery date arrived, the Depression had affected the economy, and the City was not able to pay for it.

The statue remained in the foundry yard until it was bought in 1956 by the Lincoln Park Cemetery in Bladensburg, Maryland, a suburb of Washington, D.C. It can be seen from several vantage points in a central area on their grounds.

The President is portrayed sitting in a big chair made to look like plain blocks of timber, with a shawl thrown back from his shoulders and drawn between his knees. His bared head looking downward as though brooding over problems he must solve.

In 1952, F. Lauriston Bullard of the Rutgers University Press wrote of Andrew: "O'Connor was a gifted artist of high competence in an extensive range of subjects and styles. It has been said that his work often is conceived in the most exquisite elegance and then again he creates subjects shrouded in phenomenal and impressive gloom." One is drawn to stare at this seated Lincoln for a long time, as the tiredness and sadness in his face, circles under his eyes and drooping head make one realize fully the terrible burden he carried." On a plaque next to the statue is written:

> *This statue of the great Emancipator*
> *portrays in his last days the thin, tired,*
> *war-worn president in thoughtful and*
> *deep meditation and is considered one*
> *of the finest bronze statues ever made*
> *of President Lincoln.*

A plaster version of the seated Lincoln was exhibited in the Salon in 1930. Later an oversize or heroic bust of Lincoln was sculpted for the City of London. Unveiled at the Royal Exchange by the Lord Mayor, this bust was carved from a block of American limestone, quarried near Lincoln's birth site. A similar Lincoln bust is also located in the Metropolitan Museum in New York, and El Museo de Arte de Ponce in Puerto Rico.

Now that the commission for the doors had become a certainty, Father Earls released the news to the Worcester Telegram with an accompanying picture of St. Patrick's Cathedral. The New York papers soon picked up the story.

President Abraham Lincoln.   Bladensburg, Maryland.

On April 27, O'Connor wrote Father Earls that he had been working night and day for the past two months on designs for the doors and that now they were finished. He had the doors planned for seven porches. On the East side, the *Porch of the Apostles* and the *Porch of St. Patrick.* In the north and south towers were the *Porch of the Guardian Angels* and the *Porch of the Laymen.* At the south transept was the *Porch of the Holy Virgin,* and at the north transept, the *Porch of the Saints and Heroes;* about three hundred figures in all. O'Connor went on to say that he had never done anything as fine before in his life, and although he was very tired, he wanted Fr. Earls to be the first to know... As ever, he was looking forward to seeing his friend in the near future.

On April 15, Gertrude Vanderbilt Whitney returned from France on the liner Olympic. On the trip over she planned a speech for a dinner in her honor on April 30. At the dinner, she was seated at the speaker's table between New York State Supreme Court Justice Cotillo, presiding officer, and her old friend ex-ambassador Ogden Hammond. When Gertrude finished her speech, a message was read by a representative of his Eminence Patrick Joseph Cardinal Hayes. One wonders if the conversation at the table involved St. Patrick's doors, and whether, in fact, she had been the anonymous donor whose money was to pay for their restoration.

Gertrude had been in Europe when the news release reported that the commission was granted to O'Connor. She may not have been aware of it before she returned and the money for the doors may have suddenly dried up at that dinner.

Andrew sailed to the United States in high spirits sometime near the end of June. He had completed designs for all of the doors - a task that had taken months. He was justifiably proud of his work, and very anxious to show it to the architects, and finally begin the manual work involved.

Whoever had the responsibility of breaking the news that the commission was no longer his, had a very sad task indeed. If one's heart could break, Andrew's most certainly would have at this point. With little money and no further reason to

Right. Recuillement. Thomas Mem.
Posed by Jesse Phoebe Brown..
Sleepy Hollow Cemetery.
Tarrytown, New York.

stay in the United States, Andrew booked passage on the S.S. Majestic to return to France in July. During O'Connor's short stay in New York, Maurice Reidy took his family to meet and visit with him briefly. More important however, O'Connor spent a long time talking with Father Earls. Confession being good for the soul, his dear friend was able to give him good counsel and save his sanity after this enormous disappointment. He had been depending on these doors to take care of his financial future, for he was reaching the age when he was tiring more easily from his stone carving.

On board the S.S. Majestic, O'Connor wrote to Fr. Earls: "My affairs have developed in the most agreeable manner - but one of my joys was to see you, and when all is said, it was perhaps the happiest event for me, of all. You will, I know, rejoice with me that I now turn architect and have made a contract to design and build a small church." He went on to say that he had ten years to build the church, which would contain eight statues. "This letter is simply to tell you I'm sorry I couldn't see you again, but with the immense amount of work before me and knowing how fast my working days are passing, I must hasten, so I may live to do what I've set myself to complete."

One of the greatest gifts that Andrew O'Connor Jr. possessed was that he could leave sad events behind. He always looked ahead. It is certain that Jesse shared his pain and sympathized with his fall from extreme optimism and joy to complete disappointment. Mixed with this sadness was a secret relief that the affair of so many years was now officially over and her husband could now be completely true to himself and to her.

Almost a year later, after receiving a book of poems written by Father Earls, Andrew wrote, "It's a beautiful thing when one reads your poems - to see how firm is your faith and feel how strong and happy you are in it, and it's given you the power of music to sing in unison with the birds and to understand the language of the trees."

He noted that many things had been happening to him. He was exhibiting his *Descent from the Cross* at the Salon, and also a model of his Commemorative Chapel.

Justice.
Permission of the Carnegie Foundation,
The Hague, Netherlands, and Studio of
Dick Brouwer bv. Gravenhage, Netherlands.

He had been asked to model a statue of the "Liberator", Daniel O'Connell for a bank in Dublin. It would be unveiled in 1932 at the Eucharistic Congress which was meeting for the first time in Ireland. The best thing that happened to O'Connor in 1931 was being listed in the Salon catalog as a member of the Societe des Artistes Francais.

Two months later, in July, O'Connor and Jesse prepared to go to Dublin for a month. Excited about the Daniel O'Connell statue he wanted to remind Father Earls that the unveiling would be the following May. He invited him to visit them in the house they were leasing in Dublin, assuring him there would be plenty of room.

In 1932, A year later on May first, Andrew wrote to Father Earls to tell him how sincerely sorry they all were that he wouldn't be able to come to the Congress. They had rented Leixlip Castle from the 5th of May on, and they hoped that he would come for a visit later in the summer if he couldn't be there for the celebration. Leixlip, which means "salmon's leap," was originally owned and named by the Danes when Salmon were plentiful in the stream next to the castle. Patrick thought that the most unique feature of the castle was that it was inhabited by ghosts. Coincidently, Andrew had been working for some time on a statue that he named *Ghosts*. While they were in Dublin, O'Connor planned to work and took his *Descent from the Cross* with him.

This was a very exciting time in Ireland. Great preparations were being made for the religious gathering of people from all over the world. Daniel O'Connell was a Gael; he had spoken Gaelic since he was a child, and had been raised in a Gaelic cottage, through the ancient custom of "fosterage." His family had settled in Kerry, Derryvane, after they lost all of their money and possessions. They lived very well nevertheless, by smuggling.

O'Connell was 'out of the ordinary', handsome, with an imposing presence and a voice like thunder. In the open air it could reach, allure, and captivate enormous crowds. He was able to lead the Irish people, they trusted him, and felt that he was one of them and could speak for their wants. It was considered slavery in the 1800's to be a Catholic. He used the feeling of being downtrodden to inspire people to follow him. O'Connell founded the Catholic Association of 1823, with rules cleverly drawn up to prevent it coming under a legal ban. He was a skillful lawyer, proud that he could drive a coach and six through any act of English Parliament. O'Connell's fight was with those English who recognized only the Anglican religion, never saw the misery in Ireland, and only sent agents to collect rent and taxes from the Irish.

Daniel O'Connell opposed their policies, becoming the founder of the First National Bank of Ireland. The statue, commissioned by the bank, was completed in 1932 at Leixlip Castle. It was to be unveiled at the Eucharistic Congress.

In a letter to Father Earls, Andrew wrote; "We're very sorry you're not here for this magnificent outburst of faith and enthusiasm. Nothing like it, I'm sure, has been seen in the modern world. "All Ireland as well as great numbers from the outside world are in Dublin, which is one mass of flags and banners. We have a number of guests at the castle which is only ten miles from Dublin, but we will not be content until you come over for a visit. The French Cardinal Verdier called on us yesterday, and I enjoyed one of the best hours of my life. He is a very wise and gentle man with a great love of art... We send you all our best wishes."

O'Connor, like his friend Rodin at the unveiling of his statue of Balzac, was not prepared for the vehemence with which the public greeted his *O'Connell* statue. The expectations of the huge throng were high for a traditional statue of Daniel O'Connell. When the unveiling took place, there was first astonishment, and then anger. Many said that it didn't look like any of the pictures they had seen of O'Connell. Others thought it a blasphemy. Sculpted in the manner of Rodin, O'Connell was shown with his warts and defects. Even though Andrew remembered Rodin's similar experience with his statue of Balzac, he found it extremely difficult to accept this outpouring of criticism. He thought the statue captured the essence of the great orator and statesman, and was stung by

Daniel O'Connell.
The Liberator.

122.   Christ the King or The Triple Cross.
Dun Laoghaire, Ireland.

the outcry. He packed his equipment, and fled back to Paris with Jesse. During the mid 1920's, Andrew had started a monument that he called *The Triple Cross,* as a memorial to those who died in the World War. Intending to work on it during the summer in Ireland, he finished it back at home. When it was exhibited at the Paris Salon of 1926, it had not been designed for any particular site.

He named his statue *Christ the King* when he heard that the people of Ireland desired a monument to be erected in Dun (Leary) Laoghaire the "Gateway to Ireland". It was to be a token of their unfaltering fidelity of the Faith of their forefathers and their unswerving loyalty to Christ the King of Nations. O'Connor's Cross was to become, in his own words, "the symbol of Irish faith." There is neither front nor back to this monument. The story of the faith of a people unfolds itself around the Tree of Life. The symbolism is significant; one side of the Cross shows the *Crucifixion*: Christ under a darkening cloud: the second side is named *Consolation;* Christ resurrected, completely restored, arms out-stretched to all mankind; the third is *Triumph*; Christ in majesty emerging from the tomb. Sometime in the 1930's, *The Triple Cross* was cast in bronze outside Paris at the foundry of Alexis Rudier at Malakoff. A committee of prominent laymen and clergy proposed that this sculpture would make a most fitting monument to Christ the King. The idea was a good one, but the money to pursue it was not forthcoming. The statue remained in Paris until the beginning of World War II.

As the Germans advanced toward Paris, O'Connor, Rod and Patrick dug a large hole in the foundry yard and buried the statue in three pieces in order to protect it from confiscation by either friendly military authorities or the enemy. Its valuable metal needed for arms.

The monument was dug up when the war ended, after O'Connor's death. In 1949 it was offered as a gift to the town of Dun Laoghaire. The town rejected it as unsuitable, and it lay abandoned for some time in the People's Park in Dun Laoghaire in two open crates. Eventually the sculpture was removed from the Park and taken to the home of the Archbishop of Dublin, in Drumconda. After a brief time with the Archbishop, it was removed to the back garden of a member of the secular committee. From 1968 on, several attempts were made to have the statue erected either in the National Gallery or elsewhere. Finally, the incumbent Archbishop of Dublin, Dermot Ryan, stated that he had no objection to the erection of the monument. In December of 1978, almost fifty years after its conception, *Christ the King* was erected in Dun Laoghaire, Ireland in a perfect place - in the park next to the sea.

O'Connor finally finished the statue of the *Ghosts* in the nineteen thirties. Emerging from the permanence of stone or death, they have returned to earth for some unknown reason, wishing they could rest in peace. The three figures are standing on a flight of stairs, lacking the strength to hold their bodies straight, depending on each other for support. Their faces are resigned to their fate as though they can't find peace any-where.

As Maurice Reidy interpreted: "There is no blood, no gore, and strangely, no grotesqueness. The effect is one of - sadness. O'Connor throws away the..grotesqueness so often used by Rodin. Had Rodin done *Ghosts*, he probably would have put expressions of torment and excruciating pain on their faces. O'Connor is on his own here, this is 'his' style." *Ghosts* is now at the Tate Museum.

In the spring of 1932 the London Daily News reported that O'Connor was at work in Paris on a design for a figure of Christ that would stand one hundred feet tall, to be erected at the entrance to Dublin harbor. In a letter of January 1933, to Father Earls, O'Connor mentioned that this monument was abandoned due to the lack of money required for a statue of this size.

The O'Connors had once again changed their address. They now resided at 50A Glebe Place, Chelsea, a suburb of London. This was where Andrew could find the most work and his main reason for the move. In a letter to Father Earls, Andrew mentioned that they had hopes of seeing him in Ireland the previous year, but, after two weeks or so they decided to leave, yearning for the city. - It was too soon to tell his friend about his hurt with the O'Connell rejection.- The boys had returned to Paris. He and Jesse missed them. He spoke about the weather in London being dark and cold, asked about Maurice Reidy, saying that he hadn't heard from him for a long time, and closed with his usual best wishes.

Ten months later, in October, his letter to Father Earls mentioned that it had been so long since he'd heard from him. There was much to chat about: "We came to London last November - nearly a year ago. I've got a good studio, but London is a big place to conquer - especially when one is no longer 30 years old. Of course I lived here when I was young - some 40 years ago, but although the city itself has changed but little - the few people I knew then have disappeared. I work harder than ever but the fatigue of cutting great blocks of stone begins to discourage me." He complained that his *Descent from the Cross* had worn him out, and it probably would be the last big block of stone he would do by himself. He lamented that the cost of crossing the ocean had become so great it was almost impossible to take a holiday to see others these days. The letter ended with the thought that "we go on in London not too badly."

Father Earls of Holy Cross College had many friends everywhere in the world. A kind, intelligent man who wrote poetry as a hobby, he was always helpful to everyone. There could not have been a better friend to Andrew, and they corresponded for many years. In a letter to him in January of 1934, O'Connor thanked him for sending the reviews of Eugene O'Neill's latest play. Andrew was not a reader, unless the book pertained to the subject he was sculpting, Then he read everything he could find in order to better understand the figure he was portraying. This particular letter was rather despondent. He was not impressed with English actors playing Shakespeare, or the new Shakespeare Theatre that had recently been built. He said it couldn't hold a candle to a Louis Sullivan design. Apparently, he was thinking of Louis who had died in the spring of 1924. - He greatly missed Paris, but realized if he did go back, things would have changed and there was never much work there. Enclosed in his letter was a picture of *Descent from the Cross*, which he suggested Father Earls could give to his friend O'Neill. "I'm sorry none of my works go to America, but I have so lost touch with everything there that I'm obliged to go from place to place over here looking for work." He rued the year that was wasted in Ireland by the committee who wanted to build a colossal monument near the harbor, and a St. Patrick for Gaul... "I wonder, did you ever see anything of the O'Connell I did for Dublin - or hear of the riots when the bronze was unveiled? Although it is in some ways the best statue I ever made and infinitely the best work ever seen in Ireland." He went on in his depressed state, saying that he had shaken the dust of Ireland "off my feet," and he was glad he didn't have to live there.

Father Earls took the letter with a grain of salt, knowing that everyone has a day when he chews over all his problems. He attached a note to the letter before filing it away, saying he blamed the wintry weather, the economy, and the difficulties of selling art works at a time when everyone was hurting financially. Father Earls knew that O'Connor loved Ireland, and that he wrote in a frustrated moment. He decided he would probably send O'Neill the picture of the *Descent from the Cross* and hoped that O'Connor would get a good honorarium from the National Gallery.

Little more than two months after his last letter to Fr. Earls in April of 1934 O'Connor received a letter and then a wire from him. They both told him about the statue that was to be commissioned to honor Father Francis P. Duffy, who had recently died. O'Connor replied immediately in the affirmative. He was very happy to do this, and was extremely appreciative of Father Earls' efforts.

When he was wired an invitation by the Committee in charge of the commission in New York, he immediately responded, accepting the invitation: "I will give the best that is in me upon a work for this good man and great priest."

126.

Father Duffy served as an Army Chaplain in World War I, where he rose from first lieutenant to major for heroism in the front lines. Without any regard for his own safety, he went from one first aid station to another, from one hospital to another, often cheering and encouraging the wounded. He would stop to help carry stretchers when there wasn't enough help. All the men with whom he served, loved and respected him, among them his best friends William Donovan called Wild Bill, and Alexander Woolcott. "Father Duffy is worth ten military commanders", declared Marshal Henri Gouraud, Commander of the Fourth French Army in the first World War.

When he was being feted and praised in 1921 at the 25th. anniversary of his ordination, he smilingly addressed the company: "Being bumped early and often - that's what makes you understand other people's troubles. Encouragement is all well enough, but you must dig up something from within the man if he is really to triumph."

On his return to the U.S., his parish covered New York City, where he befriended lost youngsters. In 1925 Father Duffy was elected president of the Catholic Summer School at Cliff Haven and worked hard to ensure the success of the boys' camp that bore his name.

Once when speaking about his experiences in the war, he said: "I was not a chaplain to the Catholics alone. A man can't go sticking his religion under the nose of people who do not belong to it, but so far as they want service, and very often they do, a man can do a great deal, and then in a variety of ways."

Alexander Woolcott remembered as he sat at the funeral Mass for Father Duffy in St. Patrick's Cathedral, a desperate October in 1918 when Father Duffy's regiment was cut to ribbons in the Argonne. He wrote in the New Yorker Magazine, "Especially, I recalled the black day when Colonel Donovan was carried out of the battle on a blanket. 'Wild Bill', who was the very apple of the Padre's eye. Father Duffy had always scolded him for his gaudy recklessness, and there was Father

Duffy in the dressing station. 'Wild Bill' had just strength enough left to shake a defiant fist, "Ah there, Father," he said, "you thought you'd have the pleasure of burying me!".

Father Duffy shook a fist in reply, 'and I will yet,' he said. But it was not to be that way", Woolcott went on, "for here, 14 years later was 'Wild Bill' and a thousand others of the old regiment coming up the Avenue to bury Father Duffy." Colonel Bill was appointed chairman of the Father Duffy Memorial Committee. Although William J. Donovan, was appointed chairman, all of the correspondence relating to the monument was conducted with Edward Kelly, who had been named Secretary.

In a letter to Father Earls, O'Connor related how kind Father Duffy had once been to his son Owen and he felt he owed him for that. "On your friendship - I've come to count on that coming from an unchanging source. We often wonder when we will see you again." Andrew and Jesse spent much of their time now in the Aran Islands off the coast of Galway, where he had been lent a cottage to live in, and another for his work. He was finally finding peace of mind. He hoped to be there from June on, probably until the cold weather. He decided that if he made the statue of Father Duffy, he would do it on Aran. He and Jesse felt that although London was a great and magnificent city they would prefer to live in Dublin when they retired. He went on to say that the boys were happy in Paris and he had finished a bust of Viscount D'Abernon bought by the Tate Gallery.

On April 20 secretary Ed Kelly of the Duffy Committee wrote to tell Father Earls that an informal group of the committee had met and decided that the memorial would be erected in Times Square and it would be in uniform instead of cassock. It was rather odd that on April 25th, the chairman of the Duffy committee, Colonel William Donovan, wrote to O'Connor as though this were the first time the subject of a statue had been mentioned In the course of the letter he asked if the $15,000 that they had raised for the monument would be acceptable. "I was not authorized to offer you the commission but was simply directed to ascertain from you whether or

128.

not you would feel yourself in a position to accept an offer from us." He closed with the statement that they had not contacted any other sculptor yet. As if he hoped O'Connor would lose interest on learning the amount being offered.

This letter prompted one from O'Connor to Father Earls, enclosing the letter he had received from Colonel Donovan, and wondering what was going on with this statue. It is inconceivable that O'Connor did not notice one of the names on the official correspondence paper of the Donovan committee. Among the twenty seven members listed as the executive committee on the left side of the letterhead, was that of General Cornelius Vanderbilt.

O'Connor loved Aran Isle even though it was completely stony. In order to farm, the hardy people who eked out a living there, had to build the stones into twelve foot walls surrounding the pastures they created with sea weed. Andrew enjoyed the story about the Aran Islanders who had made a very successful film, and in the promotion of it, went to London. He had heard of a half dozen of them having parties at the Savoy Hotel, eating dinners at the High Commissioner's residence, attending receptions, and dining at fine restaurants about town eating rich foods. In a letter to Fr. Earls he commented that "They will return to barren Aran - with their habits destroyed - the austerity of their lives forever ruined, as disappointment and regret take the place of their former courage in the face of adversity."

On May 17, a letter from the committee to Father Earls stated that they had just received a cable from O'Connor accepting the commission. They planned to have a meeting the following Monday, when, Mr. Kelly hoped, all details would be settled. On May 22, 1934, Kelly sent another letter to Father Earls with advance information about the statue. The commission was to definitely go to O'Connor. The chairman would be drawing up the agreement for signing.

The memorial would be erected in Times Square, and the figure clothed in the uniform of Chaplain of the U.S. Army. The unveiling was discussed, but there was no definite decision at that meeting on the date it would take place. They were all waiting for Colonel Donovan's signature. Father Earls wrote the good news to O'Connor as soon as he heard. Andrew received the cable at the end of May about the forthcoming contract. A letter came from Colonel Donovan on June 17 and O'Connor was happy that it was finally settled.

Whenever he wrote to Father Earls, Andrew tried to entice him to come to London or Ireland, but to no avail. In the letter of June 18, 1934, he mentioned that they would be on Aran Island for the next two months and discussed all of the different ways of getting there from Boston. He always hoped he could inspire the good priest to accept their hospitality. He thanked Father Earls for the publicity he had generated over the years in the Worcester paper and "while I think of it - if you know of anyone flattering me by writing an article on my work - please don't allow them to associate my name with the Columbus Monument in Spain."

He wrote of his sympathy for Father Earls on the death of his dear friend Father Kimball and offered to design something in his memory, not for money, but "as a gift perhaps - from you." He ended, "It's surprising where time goes -or is it we that go?"

O'Connor wrote Father Earls every month. In August, very excited about the trip they were planning to Aran, he gave the priest the address, hoping he would be able to visit them that year. "Colonel Donovan is, I believe, somewhere in Europe, and I think it likely we will meet in Ireland, but I don't know where. I'll be happy to see him after all you've told me of your friendship with him." He mentioned that he had seen Maurice Reidy a few times in London. Reidy had traveled from there to Ireland. Once again he cautioned Father Earls about associating his name with the Columbus Monument. Apparently, this had been on his mind after noticing the name of General Vanderbilt on the letters from Kelly. He finished his letter with the thought "... In spite of the infernal noise of war, murder, and outrage from the continent, it is quiet in London with its inhabitants going tranquilly about their affairs and no crying signs of poverty."

130.

O'Connor's September letter to Fr. Earls was an interesting travelog of Ireland. Thankfully, he had something to occupy his mind. Colonel Donovan had written him a note in June saying he would try to be in Aran, but hadn't been seen or heard from in the months following. Nothing had come from his committee either. O'Connor mentioned that he was now working on an eight foot tall statue of the Holy Virgin, indicating that he was not without work or money.

He continued in his letter; "If anyone could trouble on a quiet day to cross from Galway to Aran, supposing such a day ever happens, I can imagine nothing in the world more interesting and beautiful than such a a voyage...the wildness of the rock and the great beauty of the sky and sea added to the splendid character of the people, all make it the best holiday I have ever had in my life."

In October, after Maurice Reidy returned home from a trip to Ireland, O'Connor wrote him from London, lamenting the fact that he, Reidy, had gone through Ireland too quickly to really enjoy the country properly... "but some day, when business gets better and you are full of money... come to Galway, by some cheap and nasty steamer and I'll meet you there, spend the days with a soaking rain down your neck and in your boots, slipping over the cobblestones, at the pig or cattle market---listening to the blarneying of as reckless, unscrupulous a lot of traders as could be found cheating each other in any place in the world. And in the various bars, pubs, and hotels of which the town is full - listen to the best conversation to be heard anywhere. Would that tempt you? Well perhaps not, and yet for my part I enjoy it."

In his November letter to Father Earls, he concentrated on the weather in London, which was foggy, depressing, and un-happy. The fog in those days smelled of coal and oil, and sometimes he found himself fighting a strong urge to flee to the south of France. His work, however, was in England. Two days after Christmas, Kelly of the Father Duffy Memorial Committee, wrote Father Earls, answering his letter of a month or more and apologized. He reported that Patrick O'Connor had been in New York the first of December, and had called on Colonel Donovan. Unfortunately, Donovan was leaving for Washington almost immediately and could not spend any time with him. It seemed that the biggest mistake made on the Duffy memorial was to give the chairmanship to one who was not able to make a decision.

Kelly, however had gathered together all the information that he thought necessary for the erection of the memorial. He was happy to give it all to Patrick, who promised that his father would have a sketch in the hands of the committee after the first of the year. Kelly was surprised that O'Connor preferred working from a sketch rather than a model. He saw no problem with this however, and he replied that as soon as the sketch was received, he would submit it to the Fine Arts Commission of the City of New York for their approval, and return it immediately to O'Connor. Patrick assured Kelly that the statue would be ready for unveiling on the third anniversary of Father Duffy's death on June 26, 1935. Kelly invited Father Earls to the unveiling.

Patrick had tried to see Father Earls while he was in New York, but was disappointed to find that he was away. He then returned to London, gave the information from New York to his father and continued on to France, leaving O'Connor to begin work on the Father Duffy statue.

Andrew was saddened to receive word that Cass Gilbert, another of his friends who had steered commissions his way, had died at the age of 84. His design for the U.S. Supreme Court was under construction at his death. Many times he was responsible for getting Andrew work and O'Connor had made a portrait bust of Gilbert earlier in his life.

In his letter to Father Earls in the middle of April, 1935, O'Connor wrote: "You would hardly remember that a few hours on the train could transport you to this country, Ireland, where little or nothing resembles London. Here is the most beautiful, clean city covered by the loveliest sky you ever saw. The streets filled with handsome women - all of them laughing in spite of the fact that a great and troublesome strike is on and that rumors of political strife are filling the air and that perhaps fighting will take place on Easter day or shortly after.

"No place that I know on this earth has such reason to rejoice as this one, on the many virtues it enjoys, for I assure you a woman - let alone a man - could walk from north to south or from east to west with an open purse in his hand without so much as a finger being raised against him..." He closed saying that they would be leaving for London the following day.

On the fifth of May the Duffy memorial became history. O'Connor had endured enough procrastination and evasion. His letter to Father Earls explained that he had sent sketches to Ed Kelly, secretary of the committee, who in turn, gave them to the N.Y. Art commission. One of the art commissioners was an architect who not only could not understand the sketches, but had no idea how to build a pedestal from them. Instead of doubting the architect, in favor of a seasoned artist, Donovan found this the excuse he had been waiting for - to cancel the commission.

When O'Connor was notified of this, he angrily returned the contract as well as all the material that had been given him to aid in the work. "You will understand, I'm sure that I have neither time nor desire, to propitiate vicious and shyster members of art commissions. I make my work as well as God allows me to - and I am either right or wrong - but I do not compromise, and I am not in the trade. My business is with one higher than committees and has but little to do with jobs, and to this one alone, I answer for my work." He maintained that he was creating what he considered one of his finest statues, and he was very sorry that it wouldn't be set up in public. Always looking ahead, he and Jesse were making plans to return to Galway in a month or two.

For several years O'Connor had wanted to give Father Earls a small statue and pedestal to honor the memory of his great friend Father Kimball of Holy Cross. Once again he asked when he should send it.

Father Earls was extremely disappointed that O'Connor had not been given the commission that had involved a year of letter writing and cables and had been definitely promised the year before. He wrote to Alfred E. Smith the president of the Empire State Inc. who was in charge of the Commission, and sent along a copy of the last letter from O'Connor.

Smith didn't know anything about the situation. His position on the committee was to raise the money for the monument. "I....heard that Mr. O'Connor was not anxious to do the work and that is absolutely all that I heard about it so I got in touch with Colonel Donovan and told him I thought we ought to return the money to the people who had contributed if we were not ready to go ahead." He felt that since a year and a half had already been wasted they should get at it. Donovan asked Smith to take charge of the situation. Smith called some members of the committee, and the decision was made to give it to another sculptor. The man had already begun work on it. Father Earls had no choice but to accept Smith's explanation and send the letter to Andrew. In June O'Connor wrote to Father Earls, thanking him for the copy of the letter from Al Smith. His opinion on the matter was that, "Some people who want a monument aren't particular as to what it looks like; they just want a monument, and would be quite satisfied with whatever they got." He may have known that the statue was not to be his from the beginning. Whatever part Gertrude's relative, General Cornelius Vanderbilt, played in the ultimate decision of the Duffy committee, is speculative.

O'Connor wrote that he was looking forward to the new book of poems that Father Earls was in the process of publishing. His letter went on, "Some time ago I was called to Belfast where a committee had been formed to erect a memorial on top of a great hill, where it is said St. Patrick said Mass on one of his first days in Ireland. On the other side of the road at the foot of the hill are lakes, Patrick's purgatory, St. Patrick's Well, and nearby a tower covered with a flat rock, and in a chapel the original stone that served as St. Patrick's first altar. This place is called Saul. After a great effort in the face of a blinding wind, I arrived at the top of the hill, followed by hundreds of the inhabitants. Gathered from all the surrounding country, was a pile of rocks, and I was solemnly assured they had been placed there shortly after St. Patrick's death. It was a grand

and impressive country. I designed a monument for the site, but the secretary of the committee, for reasons best known to himself, decided to employ an Englishman to carry it out. That they stole my general design appeared to them a matter of no consequence." Money was very tight and although they wanted the best work available, most people decided to settle for what they could afford. "Returning to Dublin along the coast through a gap in Mourne Mountains was magnificent. I sometimes wonder if we Irish are not today, as great pagans as when St. Patrick arrived.

"To see a great mass of people climbing a windswept hill, in the midst of a drenching rain, with great, beautiful clouds rising and falling, often obscuring the hilltop, all with a look of divine inspiration on their faces. The old and feeble as strong in spirit as the young. All stirred by a powerful, irresistable love of the beauty of Nature. For art, architecture, sculpture or painting, I think the Irish care nothing at all, and there are no signs of any in modern Ireland." (1935)

There is no doubt that Andrew O'Connor Jr. dearly loved the land of his father, where the solitude allowed his artistic mind to flourish and he didn't have to be concerned with business or money. He finished his letter with the wish that he could be back in Ireland, for he was now 61 years old and the problems associated with the work he loved were becoming difficult.

Though he was basically an optimistic man, O'Connor had his moments of depression. In April he wrote, "For the longest time past I've been about to write you a note, but every day carries its handful of troubles and activities and - I am almost aftaid to admit it - my energies are perhaps softened - not only by the passing years - but by the immensely dull and stupid - but equally vicious civilization in which - God's eyes being turned away from me - I am forced to live, going from place to place for work. I work all the time - harder than I ever did in my life - and am happy that I'm able to." He noted that he was sending a little modern art, bronze Madonna he had made, along with the column of a sixteenth century church destroyed at the time of the separation of the Church and French State. A beautiful stone original of that century.

Instead of a Christmas card, a letter on December 21 wished Father Earls their best for Christmas and the New Year with the thought that Christmas comes a lot faster as one ages, but his mind was filled with ideas for new projects. He complained finally, that "It's a queer world we're living in and I daresay a difficult and disgusting place, where every ignorant jack in office thinks because he holds the purse strings he therefore calls the tune, forgetting that he is only what the artist makes him.

" Regard the world today. The two greatest artists living - montebanks and clowns - Hitler and Mussolini - lead the world by its nose and into a ditch." He described London, where children were running around carrying rifles and putting feathers in their hats, speeding around in cars and planes, getting ready for war.

Although he did love London, he thought that an occasional trip to Dublin was the best medicine for both he and Jesse. "In spite of everything, London - if not all of England - is in a prosperous condition and as far as one can see, prosperity is here to stay and disastrous as the climate is at this time of the year - it is still a pleasant place to live.

The O'Connors had lived at 50A Glebe Place for five years or more and apparently it suited Jesse, who was tired of moving the household furniture from place to place.

In March the mail brought a manuscript of Father Earls' "Memories". It was reviewed earlier by the "The Independent" of Dublin. Andrew cut out the review to send to Father Earls. It wasn't long until he had read the manuscript...."with your kind face before me thinking that all these names and all their owners would now be long forgotten but for the impressions made upon your mind. They strode their little stage and played their little parts and have passed on into that oblivion which awaits much greater men.

If there were more letters in 1936, there is no record, perhaps because Father Earls was not able to put them in his files, or Andrew was involved with projects that took up his time and didn't write. Andrew and Jesse surely sent their annual

Christmas greetings in December. Father Earls was in good health after Christmas and went on a trip to New York in January. He finished his business in New York and was about to leave for the middle west when, on the last day of January 1937, he died suddenly of a heart attack. Described as a "Hail fellow - well met", he liked everyone and had numerous famous friends. His job at Holy Cross was in public relations and he was well suited for it.

Maurice Reidy wrote to Andrew to tell him the sad news. It was three months before O'Connor could bring himself to answer Reidy's letter and accept the fact that his dearest friend and confidante was no longer alive. Father Earls had tied Andrew to the country he loved most. There was no male figure left in the world to share his innermost joys and tribulations without judgement. He would miss Father Michael Earls.

On May 14, 1937 in a letter to Maurice Reidy, he noted the death of Father Earls with the typical understatement he always had for things painful for him to face...."I was glad to get your letter although it contained the sad news of the death of Father Earls. He was a decent man, and although he knew or strongly suspected that I was anti-clerical, we remained friends for many years. May he rest in peace." He went on to say that he very seldom got any news from America, as he no longer had any contacts there. D.C. French had died; Stanny, St. Gaudens, Sullivan, Gilbert and most of all his father, were all gone and his boys were living in Paris.

In 1937 the Tate Gallery exhibited O'Connor's *Descent from the Cross* and *Ghosts* in their Duveen Wing. The new Queen, Elizabeth attended the exhibition and was very enthusiastic about the *Ghosts* statue.

Perhaps Maurice Reidy was not a letter writer, but at any rate, all communication from Andrew O'Connor ceased in 1937 with his last letter to Reidy. England declared war on Germany in 1938 and it was during the time London was being bombed daily, that the O'Connors moved to Dublin. Patrick found a fine town house on Merrion Square, just off the center of town, and near the National Gallery of Art.

The large stone group *Descent from the Cross* was bought in 1937 by the National Gallery of London making this five of O'Connor's works owned by this museum. He had commissions for as many portrait busts as he could handle, but found he was becoming increasingly tired. In his last years he sculpted a self portrait in marble, following the style he had adopted in his later years. This bust was 24.5 inches high. The statue was presented to the Dublin Municipal Gallery by his family following his death.

Andrew O'Connor Jr., who ranked foremost among the world's sculptors, died at his home on Merrion Square, Dublin, Ireland on Monday June 9, 1941. He had completed the circle that his father began when he was born in Ireland almost a hundred years before.

There are differing opinions about O'Connor's later works; the Duffy portrait bust, his self portrait and the Daniel O'Connell full figure bronze. Although O'Connor always remarked on the completion of a sculpture, "This is my best work ever!" these were not considered by some to be as good as his other work. The busts were similar to the Rodin style but perhaps reflected some of the bitterness he experienced after dealing with the clerics. Surely his rift with Mrs. Whitney affected his work as well.

In an interview with a reporter of the Boston Sunday Post in 1927, about his Barry statue - and it also applied to his Daniel O'Connell, "I made Barry as he really was - a rough and ready sea fighter. At that time....it was the fashion to look down on virile and vigorous statues, and unless we made the old heroes look slick, people turned up their noses. The American idea has changed since then, thank God, and we make people look like they really were."

The last ten years of Gertrude Whitney's life were not the happiest for her, either. Her husband Harry died shortly after her rift with Andrew and she turned to writing without gaining the success she desired. Pictures of her in these later years show a marked change in facial expression and aging, brought on in part by health problems and by the stress of legal battles she engaged in with her sister in law. The unhappiness she suffered from her estrangement with Andrew was not easy to forget, they had been together for many years. In the last ten years of her life she spent much of her time and energy in the Whitney Art Gallery that evolved over the years to become the Whitney Museum. It is unfortunate that these two talented people could not have broken their ties amicably and at least remained friends. Gertrude lived less than a year after Andrew. She died on April 18, 1942.

Jesse lived out her life in Dublin, surviving Andrew by thirty three years. Every afternoon in her later years, she dressed in her best clothes, topped off with a long set of pearls, wound her long, lush, auburn hair into a bun, and took a trolley to town. There she visited her favorite tea room, had tea and crumpets and then headed home. She died in Dublin on February 19, 1974 at the age of ninety six or eight. She was wont to fabricate her age, so there is some question as to the exactness of it. .Jesse was a strong spirited, lovely woman. Patrick and Roderick fondly called her by her first name, as did her grandson. Very vain about her hair, she bragged that it was long enough to sit on, and remained always the same beautiful color. When she was interviewed, Jesse always made a point of the fact that Andrew was divorced. This was apparently a part of her life she could not forget.

A few years after the second World War, a van arrived at the Paxton address and Patrick O'Connor came to the door. The stable - studio had been converted to a residence, since the main house had burned to the ground in 1929. The Chapin Fays, who owned the property spoke with Patrick, who expressed his mother's desire to see once again the place that gave her the greatest joy in her marriage. When she climbed from the van and looked around, her disappointment was evident as she exclaimed, "Nothing looks familiar." Her flower garden was gone, the studio had been razed, and the house burned. The row of blue spruce she had known as fifteen feet high had grown to five times that size, and the stripling maples had a circumference of three feet. This was the last time Jesse or Patrick ever visited Paxton.

Self Portrait of Andrew O'Connor Jr.

Patrick and Roderick were truly cosmopolitan. They lived in Florence, Paris, London, Dublin and New York. They chose to retire in Florida. The two youngest O'Connors have lived long lives, good friends always, and most delightful gentlemen in every sense of the word. They continued their painting careers, a love they developed at the ages of ten and twelve.

In 1952 Patrick was commissioned to do a bust of Commodore John Barry for the Annapolis Naval Academy library. A new library has since been built, and the bust of Barry is now in the archives.

The bronze cemetery memorial to Andrew O'Connor Sr. in Hope Cemetery, Worcester, was stolen sometime in 1991 or 1992 when the gravesite was vandalized. In Glasnevin Cemetery in Dublin, the statue *Sacred Fire,* the bronze female figure at the head of O'Connor Jr.'s grave has also been stolen.

The colossal statue of the eagle with the American soldier at St. Nazaire, France, a collaboration of Gertrude and Andrew, was destroyed by the invading German army in W.W.II. It took three of their bombs to bring it down, attesting either to the excellent design, or to poor marksmanship of the German troops.

Maurice Reidy not only kept wonderful records of Andrew Jr.'s work, but registered his own analyses of them with affection and understanding. His grandson, Michael, wrote his college thesis using the information, adding additional facts to the original work.

Helene Desmairoux's French language record of Andrew's work, clearly a labor of love, became the definitive source of information for this biography. Her comprehensive book has been quoted in articles written in the Worcester newspapers as well as the New York Times, papers in Paris and London. Researchers have also found it invaluable.

In 1974 on the one hundredth anniversary of his birth, a plaque was placed on the house on Merrion Square, Dublin, where Andrew spent his last years. The memorial was dedicated by

James White, Director of the National Gallery. Most of the statues that remained in O'Connor's studio were donated to the Dublin Municipal Gallery by Jesse and her sons, knowing that this was what he wished.

Many people eulogized him at his death, but his old friend Maurice Reidy summed it up best. "Much has been said about Andrew O'Connor and his works. However, the measure of an artist is not really how his public feels about him; whether he won awards or not - whether he was accepted or rejected by the critics really doesn't make an artist great. What makes an artist great is the way in which he views his own efforts - if he doesn't take his work too seriously and thrills in fooling the public, his art is not great regardless of what is said or written about him.

"When an artist is dedicated and puts his soul into his work and is unyielding in his cry 'this is mine, it is good, and damn your opinions, I know that this is art!' there cannot then fail to be meaning and value in this man's work."

Helene Desmairoux once wrote; "O'Connor is a thinker - dreamer - but he is also a man of action, an indefatigable worker in the labor that he loves. When he is not working, he sleeps or daydreams. If he hears a conversation about him which accords with his meditations, he talks - exposing and developing his thoughts in such simple and imaginative language that one never tires of listening to him. He is all sincerity so he will not permit himself to become entangled with words. When he can no longer express his thoughts, O'Connor becomes silent."

To repeat what Andrew Sr. once said; "The glory of man consists in the fact that he is a distinct creation, an individuality without a counterpart in all the universe. The development of this personality is his mission; if he does well his face will show it, and if he does ill, no art can hide it; in either case his preservation of it for others is a service which the various museums of the world prove they abundantly appreciate."

Father Earls and Andrew O'Connor Jr.
Probably taken at the time of his last visit
to the United States in 1930 when he was
to start the St. Patrick's Cathedral doors.

WORKS OF O'CONNOR JR.

Inspiration; Statue of young woman for St. Louis
Exposition of 1904.
Recuillement or Grief; Seated young woman - General
Thomas Memorial. Sleepy Hollow Cemetery,Tarryton,NY.
Memorial to General Henry Lawton, Garfield Park,
Indianapolis, IN.
La Fauness or the Crooked Smile, Crawford Gallery,Ir
Robert Lawfton Newman bust, Luxembourg Museum, Paris
1898 or The Spanish Soldier,Worcester,Massachusetts.
Governor John Johnson flanked by the Toilers; The
Farmer, Miner, Iron Worker and Half Blind Man:
Capitol Building, St. Paul, Minnesota.
Marble memorial to General Lew Wallace Hall of
Statues, Capitol Building, Washington, D.C.
Bronze memorial.Lew Wallace Library Crawfordsville,
Indiana..
General Mansfield bas relief; West Point Military
Academy, West Point, New York.
Jean Alphonse Monod bust; Chambery, France.
Kemal Pasha Equestrian, Istanbul, Turkey.
Sybil,A young woman, An Armful of Roses, She Dreams;
bas reliefs on the sides.of the two seated figures
Newark, NJ.
Doors ST. Bartholomew Church, New York, NY.

Loney Family Tomb door. Skaneateles, NY.
First National Bank and Trust Co. Marquette,MI.
Liberty Memorial Co. doors. Kansas City, MO.
Miner's National Bank doors. Pottsville, PA.
The Exiles.
Abraham Lincoln's Farewell Address; Springfield,
Illinois State House.
Large Lincoln Busts; Royal Exchange, London,England.
Metropolitan Museum, New York, N.Y.
El Museo de Arte de Ponce, Puerto Rico.
Seated Lincoln;Lincoln Park Cemetery,Bladensburg,MD.
Forbes Building doors. New York, NY.
Lord D'Abernon bust; Tate Museum, London, England.
Marquis de LaFayette; Washington Park, Baltimore,MD.
Maternity.
Tristan and Iseult Brooklyn Museum; Brooklyn, N.Y.
Indian Squaw. First marble, unknown location.
Italian Girl or Una Calabraise.Luxembourg Museum,
Paris,France.
Head of the Virgin bronze; Metropolitan Museum, NY.
Adam and Eve; or Temptation, Marble. Corcoran
Gallery, Washington, D.C.
Marble Crucifix;Holy Cross College Library,Worc.MA.
Andrew O'Connor Sr. bronze funeral monument.Hope
Cemetery. Worcester, Massachusetts. Since stolen..
Gorham Building facade; New York, NY.
Virgin from the marquette The Arrival; Dublin Mu-
nicipal Gallery, Dublin, Ireland.
Cass Gilbert Bust.
Statue of Virgin.- Eight foot. Ireland.

WORKS OF O'CONNOR JR.

Debarquement; Three figures; Mother or Mother of
Sorrows; Wife or the Mourning Woman and Victim.Tate
Gallery, London England,Merrion Square,Dublin Ire.
Ghosts; Tate Gallery, London, England and also
Campion House Isleworth, Middlesex, England.
The Golden Head; Tate Gallery, London, England.
The Bronze Mask; Coll.of Felix Seguine, Paris,France
Nehimiah; Budapest Czechoslovakia.
Dierdre bust; National Gallery of Ireland, Dublin..
Dante;
Virgin in Stone.
The Virgin and the Infant.
Four plaques New York City Main Library, N.Y.
Robert Emmet; Washington, D.C.
The Slave.
Judith; bas relief, Newark, New Jersey.
Madame X.
Forbes Building doors. New York, NY.
Sacre Feu or the Sacred Fire; Stolen from the grave
of Andrew Jr. in Glasnevin Cemetery, Dublin,Ireland.
Justice; Peace Palace, The Hague, Netherlands.

John Wolf Ambrose memorial,Battery Park.New York,N.Y
Edward Tuck portrait bust; Luxembourg Museum, Paris,
France. Also Concord Historical Museum, Concord,N.H.
Father Duffy bust; National Gallery, Dublin, Ire.
Self Portrait; National Gallery, Dublin,
Triple Cross or Christ the King; Dun Laoghaire, Ire.
Daniel O'Connell; National Bank of Ireland, Dublin.
The Arrival; made with Staff material. Never sold;
dismantled, parts sold separately.
The Owl; Originally in the Stanford White Collec-
tion. Now owned by Roderick O'Connor.
Fortunata; White House Collection, Washington, D.C.
Also in Reidy collection.
Col.Emerson Liscum memorial.Arlington Cemetery,VIR.
Bust of La Gloire Militaire in Metropolitan Museum.
Norcross Whitney bronze bas relief;Worc..City Hall.
Bust of Commodore Barry; Annapolis Naval Academy.
by Patrick O'Connor.
Bust of James Manson, Municipal Gallery, Dublin,Ir.
Temple Emanuel doors, New York, NY.
Strathcona or The Red Granite Head.
Many other busts not known in London and Ireland.

WORKS OF O'CONNOR SR.:1893 list of portrait
busts.

Governor S. Padelford; Rhode Island.
Governor A.H. Bullock; Massachusetts.
Hon. S. Salisbury Sr; Worcester,MA. National Bank,
Hon. G.F. Verry; Worcester, Mass.
Hon..F. Sayles; Providence, Rhode Island.
Judge Chapin; Worcester, Mass.

WORKS OF O'CONNOR SR.

Judge F.H. Dewey; Worcester, Mass.
Rt. Rev. P.T. O'Reilly; Springfield, Mass.
Rev. W.M. Parr; F.R.S.; Hope Cemetery, Worcester,Ma.
Rev. Mr. Kimmens; Southbridge, Mass.
Gen. U.S. Grant; Unknown location.

Gen Geo. H. Ward; Gettysburg, Pennsylania.
Lieut. Willie Grout; Worcester, Mass. Hist. Museum.
E.A. Goodnow; Princeton, Mass. Library.
Loring Coes; Worcester, Mass.
Mr. Penniman; Dudley, Mass.
Isaac Goulding; Worcester, Mass.
C.M. Dyer; Worcester, Mass.
Burnham Wardwell; Hope Cemetery, Worcester, Mass.

Dr.Geo.Chandler;Worcester,Mass.

W.J.Hogg; Worcester,Mass.
Mrs.L.J.Knowles,Worcester,Mass.Hospital.
Mrs.L.Coes;Worcester,Mass.
Mrs.A.C. Freeland; Worcester, Mass.
The following are busts and medallions in plastic,
which gradually becomes enduring.
Cyrus Hamlin,D.D;RobertCollege,Constantinople,Turkey
Rev.McFarland; Cathedral, Providence,R.I.
Geo.B.Cheever,D.D. Howard College, Washington D.C.
Albert Curtis; Worcester, Mass.
Gen.Charles Devens; Worcester, Mass.
Gen.Josiah Picket; Worcester, Mass
Henry T. Cheever, D.D. Bowdoin College, Maine.

Ichabod Washburn; Old Ladies Home, Worcester,Ma.
After his list in 1893, there are no other known
lists of his work..
Following is a brief list of many that O'Connor Sr.
did not document.
The Wounded Lion; Antietam Civil War Cemetery Vir.
Civil War Monument; Spencer, Mass.
Whittall Memorial; Hope Cemetery, Worcester, Mass.

The Fisher Boy; Elm Park, Worcester, Mass.

Coes Family monument; Hope Cemetery, Worcester,Mass.
Unfortunately documentation of many works of both
men was not saved.

NOTES:

A Short History of Ireland; by Roger Chauvire.

A History of Ireland; by Edmund Curtis, 1935.

P.3 & 4 Information taken from these books.

Sculpture in America; by Wayne Craven. U. of Delaware

P.3 Information from; "Florence - most of the"

P. 3 "Clay -- necessary."

P. 4 ,5. Worcester City Directory; Located Worcester
Public Library.

P.5 - 7 Bigelow and Puritan Statue; Worcester Telegram
and Gazette.(W.T.G.) Microfilm Worcester Public Library.

THE STORY OF CHICAGO; by Joseph and Carolyn Kirkland.
Published by Dibble Co. 1894.

P.10 "The Exposition....foot by foot.

P.11 "Here - six o'clock"

P.13, General information.

P.13."A gigantic.....in Chicago.

P.14 "Still an enormous....nightmare."

P,14 "The Fair....saw it.

P.16,17. General information.

AN AMERICAN SCULPTOR; DANIEL CHESTER FRENCH; by Michael
Richmond. 1975 printed by Nicholas David.

P.17,18,19.. Background Information.

P.17 "French was a modeler...what I could get here.

P.17 "During the day....to the cellar...steel syringes

P.18 "in the studio."..."A sculptor...for a site."

P.19 "It is - home."

P.19. General information.

P.19. SARGENT'S BOSTON; David McKibbon. 1956 Pub. Mus.
of Fine Arts, Boston.

P.20. "The brittle - character."

P.20. "Mrs. Sargent - return." "John - in the "

P.21. "cultural - developement."

P.21. Poem information from Patrick O'Connor.

P.23. The Wounded Lion. W.T.G. Microfilm W.P.L.

P.24. AN AMERICAN SCULPTOR; "He - Massachusetts."

P.25. "Once - touch"   "The set - in use."

P.26. "French - exists.".

STANNY, THE GILDED LIFE OF STANFORD WHITE. by
Paul R. Baker.Pub. The Free Press (div) Mac Millan Inc.

P.27. Background information.

P.27. "Corinthian - Apostles." "The completion - him."

P.27. "Thought - old man." "White - work.".

P. 32-35 General Information. LE OEVRE DU SCULPTOR
O'CONNOR. By Helen Desmairoux.

P.30. Liscum Statue information.

P.30 MAURICE REIDY RECORDS; The Loney Family Tomb.

P.30. "A series - laborers."

P.30. "On - culture." " A different - Museum."

146.

P.31. MAURICE REIDY RECORDS; Pictures of doors.
HOMAN POTTERTON CATALOG. 1974 Anniversary of death.
P.32. "Across - Mars".
P.34. Recuillement Statue. BOSTON SUNDAY POST; March 20,1927.
DICTIONARY OF AMERICAN BIOGRAPHY; 1933 General Henry
P.35. Lawton information.
P.36. POTTERTON CATALOG; Paris address. Medals.
P.35. SKETCH OF ANDREW O'CONNOR; 4/8/1915 P.6 W.T.G. Microfilm W.P.L. on Lawton dedication.
P.38,39. STANNY;
P.40. Information on Gertrude Vanderbilt Whitney.
P.40. HOMAN POTTERTON information on statues & exhibits.
P.42, 44, 45. STANNY;
P.45, 46.. Commodore Barry information; W.T.G. Microfilm in W.P.L.
P.45. "Art on our Streets and In Our Parks, by Edith Abercrombie Snow.
P.45. Design for Spencer. W.T.G. in W.P.L. 9/8/1905.
P.46, 47.. General Lew Wallace;Information from the Crawfordsville Visitor Center and Ben Hur Museum.
THE WORLD OF RODIN 1840-1917; by Harlan Hale and the Editors of Time Life Books, N.Y.
P.47,48. "A visit - work."
P.48. REIDY; "illusion - semi-completed.
P.49,51.. POTTERTON; "In 1909 - 1910.
P.49. 1911 General Alvear. L'OEVRE DU SCULPTEUR.
P. 50, 51, 52. WORCESTER MAGAZINE on Governor John Albert Johnson memorial committee. W.P.L.Worcester Room.
GERTRUDE VANDERBILT WHITNEY; By B.N. Friedman and Flora Miller Biddle, Doubleday Co.
P.54. "Gertrude - and then-"
P.54. "it's heaven". "she thought - himself." "When - a thing of."
P.55. "meaning - have found." " Of course - the other."
P.55. "He was struck - on the light."   "A fearfully - coming?"
P.55. Information taken from GERTRUDE VANDERBILT WHITNEY.
P.56. "I want - you always."
P.56.. GERTRUDE VANDERBILT WHITNEY information.
P.57,58,59,60. FRENCH LETTERS: Microfilm copies, courtesy Wanda Stycka, Chesterwood Museum, Stockbridge, MA.
P.59. POTTERTON CATALOG; Dates and sculptures.
P.60. Information from GERTRUDE VANDERBILT WHITNEY.
P.61,62. REBELS ON EIGHTH STREET. by Juliana Force and the Whitney Museum of American Art.Information about Mac Dougal Alley, New York City.
P.73,74. Worcester Sunday Telegram;1934 by Robert B. Atwood. Lincoln of the Farewell Address.

Notes;

LOUIS SULLIVAN AS HE LIVED; By Willard Connely Pub. Horizon Press Inc. N.Y. 1960.

THE IDEA OF LOUIS SULLIVAN By John Sjarkowski, Univ. Minnesota Press. Minn.

P.75. Information about Louis Sullivan.

P.76 Potterton on exhibit.

GERTRUDE VANDERBILT WHITNEY;

P.77. Information.

P.76,77,79,80. Andrew O'Connor's Boy Scout Monument by Mary Evans. W.T.G. 11/19/51.

P. 81. SCULPTURE IN AMERICA;

P.82,83,84. REIDY COLLECTION.

P.84,85. POTTERTON CATALOG. Exhibits and dates.

P.84,85.. STANNY; Lunchion meeting on doors to N.Y.U.

P.86. POTTERTON CATALOG; Exhibit and statues.

P.86,87. REIDY COLLECTION. Information on Peace statue for the Hague, Netherlands.

P.88. Whittall Memorial WTG. Microfilm W.P.L. 5/29/24.

P.88,89. Worc. Sunday Telegram 12/30/23. "Sailing Away to Italy With Natives Of That Country"- A. O'Connor Sr. Worcester Historical Museum.

Letters to Father Michael Earls. Property of the Holy Cross College archives.

P.91. W.T.G. 7/22/1924. "Andrew O'Connor Sr. Dies At Holden Home." Microfilm W.P.L.

P.91. "Holy Cross Cruficix". Sun. Tel. Mag. Sect. P.1. 1/27/1924.

P.93. Andrew O'Connor Sr. Memorial in Hope Cemetery. Picture permission of Chesterwood Museum, Stockbridge, MA.

P. 92. Reidy on the Crucifix: "Christs - power."

P.93. W.T.G. Microfilm W.P.L. "President to speak at Baltimore Event." 9/1/24.

P.94. Two monuments believed to be those of O'Connor Sr.

GERTRUDE VANDERBILT WHITNEY; On St. Nazaire statue.

P.96,97. Information on St. Nazaire.

P.97. Information from: REBELS ON EIGHTH STREET. By Avis Berman. Pub. Athenium., NY.

P.98. REIDY PAPERS; On "Fortunata".

P.99. G.V.W. On Columbus.

P.99. REBELS ON EIGHTH STREET. Information. on St. Nazairre.

P100. G.V.W. On Columbus. "O'Connor visited - pieces."

P.101. G.V.W. Columbus.

P.103. G.V.W. Information on Columbus statue;

P.104. G.V.W. On Springfield, Ma. monument.

P.105. G.V.W. "Every - Back." Information on rental unit.

P.106,107. G.V.W. Information on Columbus unveiling.

P.108. MS. FLORA MILLER IRVING; Picture of Columbus statue at Huelva, Spain.

NOTES:

All letters and Telegrams property of HOLY CROSS COLLEGE ARCHIVES.

P. 114. Lincoln information. LINCOLN PARK CEMETERY, Bladensburg,MD.

P. 116. G.V.W. Information on Gertrude's dinner of April 15 in New York.

P. 120,121. "Daniel O'Connell ---- smuggling". :O'Connell ---- Catholic" A HISTORY OF IRELAND.

P.121"Association of ---- policies."

P.123. OUCAS; "Christ the King Triumphs." March 1979.Story of Triple Cross.

P. 124. REIDY; "There....their faces."

P. 127, 128. BOSTON SUNDAY POST. May 27, 1934. "Bay State Sculptor to Make Statue of FAMOUS WAR HERO - PRIEST. BY Leo Rabbette.

Acknowledgements and thanks:

Arthur Longwell, Vol. Worcester Historical Museum, Worc. MA.
James Mahoney, Archivist Dinand Library, Holy Cross College,Worc.
Worcester Public Library Volunteers and Staff.
Worcester Historical Museum Staff; Joan Bedard, Ronald Borjeson
Dir. William Wallace.
Wanda Styka, archivist Chesterwood Museum, Stockbridge, MA.
Angelo Scola, Worcester State College, Worc. MA.
The Newark Museum archivist, Newark, NJ.
James Cheevers, archivist, Annapolis Naval Academy, Annap. MD.
Donald J. Stinson, Village Historian, Skaneateles, NY.
Scott Wiggins, St. Paul, Minnesota.
Manager Glen View Country Club, Glen View, Illinois.
Walter and Phyllis Lindquist. Waukegan, Illinois.
Cleveland Art Museum, Cleveland, Ohio.
Jame Neale. Holden, MA.
Mary McInerny, Dublin, Ireland.
Homan Potterton. New York, NY.
Nancy Paddock. Rutland, MA.
Phyllis Meagher. Rutland, MA.
Mary Jane Roadstrum. Holden, MA.
Ann Borjeson. West Boylston, MA.
Kenneth Swanstrom. Worc. MA.
Phillip and Janice Reidy. Worc. MA.
W.A. Hamel, General Director, Carnegie Foundation. Netherlands.
Helena and Chris Liazos. Worc. MA.
Linda Honan, Westboro, MA.
Craig Soderman. Paxton, MA.
Ursula Kolmstetter, Indianapolis Museum of Art.

Dr. Ellen Kosmer, Westboro, MA.

Special Thanks.

Michael Reidy, grandson of Maurice, who kept all of his grandfather's records and unselfishly shared them. London, England.
Mrs. Flora Miller Irving. New York, NY.
Patrick O'Connor. Florida.
Roderick O'Connor. Florida.
Laurie Larson, always there when needed.

Lisa Larson, without whom the computer would have won the battle.

INDEX:

INDEX cont.

INDEX: cont.